Breaking the Code of the Feasts

Discover how future events are hidden in the Feasts and special celebrations of Israel.

PERRY STONE, JR.

Voice of Evangelism
Cleveland, TN

BREAKING THE CODE OF THE FEASTS

ISBN 0-9785920-4-2

Cover design: Michael Dutton

Printed in the United States of America.

Breaking the Code of the Feasts

Discover how future events are hidden in the Feasts and special celebrations of Israel.

Dedication

I wish to dedicate this book to my dear personal friend and colleague in ministry, Bill Cloud. I first met Bill when he was the youth pastor at a church in Deland, Florida. There, Bill developed an interest in Hebraic roots and through intense study and dedication has become a noted voice in this unique field. After leaving youth work, he served on my staff for three and-a-half years before beginning his own ministry. I am grateful for Bill's friendship, his research and the times we have "revelated" from God's Word as we studied the amazing Hebraic foundation of the Christian faith.

Contents

Foreword

If you are familiar with our weekly telecast Manna-fest, you are aware that the emphasis of our teaching and preaching ministry is three-fold.

- ■ To win people to Christ, and help them grow in the grace of God.

- ■ To minister a "right now" prophetic word and help discern the times and seasons.

- ■ To teach believers the Hebraic roots of their faith.

This book is more than a teaching about the Hebrew roots of our faith and more than an explanation of the Seven Feasts of Israel. The book title, *Breaking the Code of the Feasts,* gives you a clue to the content of this book. Just as the parables of Jesus contain stories hidden within a story that required an explanation by the master teacher, the feasts and special celebrations of Israel have more than just a practical meaning. They are both practical and prophetic. Each feast contains clues pointing to future events.

This is important to understand because the feasts can reveal incredible insight into what has been fulfilled through Christ and what will be fulfilled in the near future.

I have also included unique codes found in the celebrations of Hanukkah and Purim as well as unique insight into the Final Battle commonly referred to as Armageddon. Of all places, the story of Gideon is what may provide the best parallel for this coming event. All in all, this book will demonstrate the depth and inherently prophetic nature of God's Word. So, get ready for an amazing journey into the depth of Scripture and Hebraic wisdom!

Be blessed.

Perry Stone Jr.

Chapter One

OPENING THE BOOKS IN HEAVEN

"And there are also many other things that Jesus did, which if they were written one by one, I suppose that even the world itself could not contain the books that would be written. Amen." – John 21:25

It might be true that temporal books down here on earth couldn't contain all the works of Jesus, nevertheless, there are books in Heaven that not only contain what He has done, is doing and will do, but they keep a record of everything you and I have done, as well. No detail, no situation or scenario has escaped His attention. The man who penned the passage above, John, saw first hand just how magnificent and supreme God truly is and how meticulous He is when it comes to recording those things that have been, are and will be.

Born into a priestly family and last of the original twelve apostles, John eventually found himself imprisoned by Rome on the island of Patmos. While he was there, he had an experience that resulted in the book we call "the Revelation of Jesus Christ"; one of the most mysterious books in all of Scripture.

It happened that John was in the "Spirit on the Lord's day" and was caught up into Heaven. There he saw, not only visions of future events, but a glorious vision of the heavenly Throne Room and all those who were gathered there. From his description of the Throne Room of God, we know that the floor is made of clear glass that, like a crystal, changes colors from blue to red to clear.

We also know that the Throne of God has the appearance of Jasper and Sardius stone. It should be noted that Jasper and Sardius are the **first and last** stones on the breastplate of the Priest. Of course, we know that our heavenly High Priest *is* the First and the Last (Revelation 1:11).

Behind the throne there is a rainbow, the token of the covenant He made with earth and its inhabitants when He said that He would never again destroy the earth with a flood of waters (Genesis 9:11-15). Surrounding the Throne are four living creatures who cry day and night, "Holy, Holy, Holy" (Revelation 4:8) as well as twenty-four lesser thrones upon which the twenty-four elders sit (Revelation 4:4).

Among all of the indescribable features of God's Throne and the heavenly Temple, there exist some very important books; some of which are open and some of which are sealed. Let us begin our study by examining these books and their relevance to our subject.

THE BOOKS IN THE HEAVENLY TEMPLE

The Bible tells us that there are five significant books in Heaven.

- The Book of the Living
- The Book of Life
- The Book of Tears
- The Book of Works
- The Book of Remembrance

The first one, the Book of the Living, contains your personal information, the number of your days and your destiny. The Jews also call this the "Book of Destiny."

"Let them be blotted out of the book of the living, and not be written with the righteous." – Psalms 69:28

"Your eyes saw my substance, being yet unformed; and in Your book they all were written, the days fashioned for me, when as yet there were none of them." -Psalms 139:16

The Amplified Version of the Scriptures states it this way:

"Your eyes saw my unformed substance, and in Your book all the days of my life were written before ever they took shape, when as yet there were none of them." – Psalm 139:16 (AMP)

The Bible tells us there is a "Book of Tears."

"You number my wanderings; put my tears into Your bottle; are they not in Your book?" – Psalm 56:8

Even though the New Testament reveals that there are multiple "books" in Heaven, the most notable of these is the "Book of Life," also referred to as the "Lamb's Book of Life." No doubt referring to this book, Jesus said, "Rejoice because your names are written in heaven" (Luke 10:20). Apparently, even Moses knew about this book because he warned against having one's name blotted out! (Deuteronomy 29:20).

"He who overcomes shall be clothed in white garments, and I will not blot out his name from the Book of Life; but I will confess his name before My Father and before His angels." - Revelation 3:5

"And I saw the dead, small and great, standing before God, and books were opened and another book was opened, which is the Book of Life. And the dead were judged according to their works, by the things which were written in the books." - Revelation 20:12

"And I urge you also, true companion, help these women who labored with me in the gospel, with Clement also, and the rest of my fellow workers, whose names are in the book of life." - Philippians 4:3

Of the Book of Works, the Bible says:

"And I saw the dead, small and great, stand before God; and the books were opened: and another book was opened, which is the book of life: and the dead were judged out of those things which were written in the books, according to their works." - Revelation 20:12

Finally, there is the Book of Remembrance.

"Then those who feared the LORD spoke to one another, and the LORD listened and heard them; so a book of remembrance was written before Him for those who fear the LORD and who meditate on His name. They shall be mine, says the LORD of hosts, on the day that I make them My jewels. And I will spare them as a man spares his own son who serves him."
- Malachi 3:16–17

Aside from the Book of Life, this is one of the most interesting books kept in Heaven, for those who are written in this book make up "God's jewels." In Hebrew the word "jewels" is סגלה *segulah*. This is the same word that is used in Exodus to describe His people Israel just after He brought them out of Egypt.

"Now therefore, if you will indeed obey My voice and keep My covenant, then you shall be a special treasure to Me above all people, for all the earth is Mine, and you shall be to Me a kingdom of priests and a holy nation." - Exodus 19:5-6

Segulah is translated here as "a special treasure."

God's "special treasures," His "jewels" are those who obey His voice (Exodus 19:5), who fear Him and meditate upon His name (Malachi 3:16). Speaking to the believers in Jesus Christ, Peter echoes this same theme in his first letter when he says:

"But you are a chosen generation, a royal priesthood, a holy nation, His own special people, that you may proclaim the praises of Him who called you out of darkness into His marvelous light." - 1 Peter 2:9

Another important feature of this book is the fact that this is the one God refers to when it is time for Him to move on someone's behalf. The fact that it is called the Book of **Remembrance** speaks to this issue. You see, from a Hebraic point of view, "to remember" means much more than what we think of in the West.

The word *zikron*, translated as "memorial" means "a memorable thing," "a day" or "a writing." This word expresses that "something is written to remind someone to do something on a certain day." To some degree, that sounds a lot like our meaning of the word. However, when we look at the root word *zakar*, the true intent makes a deeper impression. *Zakar*, translated as "remembrance," means "to speak on behalf" of someone or something. The Bible tells us that when God "remembers" someone, something miraculous happens. Below are just a few examples of what happened to certain people when God "remembered" them.

■ He opened up Rachel's womb – Genesis 30:22

- He delivered Israel from bondage - Exodus 2:24
- He opened Hannah's womb – 1 Samuel 1:19

When God "remembered Noah" (Genesis 8:1), the Scripture wasn't inferring that God had forgotten him. No, the text is saying that, due to Noah's obedience, it had come time for God to speak on his behalf. When He began to speak on Noah's behalf, the flood waters began to abate. Oddly enough, the day on which Noah removed the cover of the ark and discovered that the surface of the ground was dry was "in the first month, the first day of the month" (Genesis 8:13). This particular day would later be known as *Yom Teruah* or the Feast of Trumpets.

The Feast of Trumpets, as it turns out, is also known as *Yom Ha Zikkaron* or the "Day of Remembrance." This is the day that God said was to be a "memorial (*zikkaron*) of blowing of trumpets" (Leviticus 23:24). It is believed that, on this day, the Book of Remembrance is opened so that God can deliver those who "fear His name."

The Purpose of the book seems to be that those whose names are written in this book are in line to receive a breakthrough in their lives or deliverance from adversity. The Bible tells us that God remembers His covenant with his people. God remembers those who fear Him. He remembers His children in time of need and delivers them in times of trouble. Apparently, it is the existence of this book that provokes Him to do these things.

For those of us in this day and time, it is important to be listed in this book because this generation faces the threat of calamity and destruction unlike anything the world has ever seen.

"For behold, the day is coming, burning like an oven; and all the proud, yes, and all who do wickedly will be stubble. And the day which is coming shall burn them up, says the LORD of hosts, that will leave them neither root nor branch." - Malachi 4:1

According to Scripture, for those whose names are written in the Book of Remembrance, there is the promise that He will deliver them when the "seals are broken" and the day of trouble strikes the earth.

THE SEVEN-SEALED BOOK IN HEAVEN

"And I saw in the right hand of him who sat on the throne a scroll written inside and on the back, sealed with seven seals. Then I saw a strong angel proclaiming with a loud voice, 'Who is worthy to open the scroll, and to loose its seals?' " - Revelation 5:1-2

There are diverse beliefs about what this seven-sealed scroll or book is, but the idea that makes the most sense to me is that it is a Divine Will or a Title Deed, if you will. As the seals are opened and certain consequences are manifest on earth, it becomes apparent that the original owner is reclaiming what is his. Considering what we have learned about the Book of Remembrance, it stands to reason that this book is related to that one; God is about to speak on behalf of His purposes and reclaim and restore the earth to His original plan and intent. God is **remembering**

His covenant with earth *and* with mankind.

That the earth is being "restored" to its original owner speaks to us of the laws concerning the *Yovel* or as we say, the Jubilee. Apparently, the opening of this sealed book initiates the Jubilee that redeems the earth from Satan's control once and for all. So then, to understand the purpose of these seals and the effects they cause on the earth, it is important that we understand what the Scripture has to say about the Jubilee.

THE LAW OF JUBILEE

"And you shall consecrate the fiftieth year, and proclaim liberty throughout all the land to all its inhabitants. It shall be a Jubilee for you, and each of you shall return to his possession, and each of you shall return to his family." - Leviticus 25:10

The theme of Jubilee was and is redemption, freedom and restoration. God established this statute for Israel so that all those who were oppressed and in tribulation were released; slaves were freed to return to their homes. For those who had fallen on hard times and had lost their land and inheritance, it meant they could legally reclaim it - with certain conditions being met - and be restored to their land. In other words, the land that had been lost to someone else was given back to the family God had originally given it to. Finally, that year was a year of rest for the people and for the land.

The laws of Jubilee were enacted after seven Sabbaths of seven years, or a total of forty-nine years. In the fiftieth year on the Day of Atonement, silver trumpets were blown to announce the Jubilee had begun. Once the trumpets had been sounded, any family that could present proof of ownership - a written will or genealogy - of a piece of property could redeem it back. If they were unable to do this themselves, they could have their next of kin – a *go el* or "kinsman redeemer" - buy back the right to the property for them.

Interestingly enough, wills in the biblical era were often sealed seven times, meaning that only someone of supreme importance was authorized to open the will. It is recorded that Caesar Augustus had his will sealed with seven seals. Tradition has it that Jewish families who lost possessions, whether it be land or other items, would itemize these possessions in a scroll sealed with seven seals. This was done so that in the time of Jubilee, they would be prepared to redeem them back.

Sometimes these scrolls had writing on the inside (referred to as *recto*) and outside (called *verso*). Some scrolls, called *opisthographs*, were written on the front and back. These types of scrolls would be similar to what the prophet Ezekiel described.

"Now when I looked, there was a hand stretched out to me and, behold, a scroll of a book was in it. Then He spread it before me, and there was writing on the inside and on the outside and written on it were lamentations and mourning and woe." - Ezekiel 2:9-10

Here is what I want you to see. After he was given the dominion over the earth (Genesis 1:26), Adam lost his inheritance to the Adversary. Nevertheless, God had already recorded in heaven who the rightful inheritor was, and had already made provisions for the "kinsman redeemer" to restore it back to its original owner. In other words, before man even knew of a Jubilee, God had already determined when it would take place; it was written in a book and then sealed until someone worthy could break the seals. Even though Satan is presently the ruler of this world (John 14:30), the kingdoms of this world must be subject to Christ. In fact, notice what happens after the seventh seal of this heavenly scroll is opened.

"When He opened the seventh seal, there was silence in heaven for about half an hour. And I saw the seven angels who stand before God, and to them were given seven trumpets. . . . So the seven angels who had the seven trumpets prepared themselves to sound."
- Revelation 8:1-2, 6

That there is a silence in heaven of about half an hour suggests this is taking place on Yom Kippur. Recall that, according to Scripture, the silver trumpets announcing the Jubilee are sounded on Yom Kippur. At the opening of the seventh seal, seven angels are given trumpets and prepare to sound them; Jubilee is about to begin. The Bible continues:

"But in the days of the sounding of the seventh angel, when he is about to sound, the mystery of God would be finished, as He declared to His servants the prophets." - Revelation 10:7

When the seventh trumpet sounds and finalizes the advent of Jubilee, the Scripture declares that "the mystery of God" is completed. In other words, all of those things that have remained hidden are being manifest in the earth. This is a very important fact for us to understand and remember. With the breaking of each of these seals, mysteries – hidden truths – are being revealed. As this revelation proceeds, God's great plans and purposes are made known to mankind.

His ultimate purpose is that the "land" - the earth - be restored to its rightful owner and heir. All lost possessions are going to be reclaimed by the one who has the power and authority to repossess them. And so, we understand that the seven-sealed book is the Title Deed to the earth. When the seals are opened and the seventh trumpet sounds, the restoration process is completed.

"Then the seventh angel sounded. And there were loud voices in heaven, saying, 'The kingdoms of this world have become the kingdoms of our Lord and of His Christ, and He shall reign forever and ever!' "
- Revelation 11:15

As you see, all of these events transpire in accordance with the laws of Jubilee. Notice that:

- The Title Deed is opened.
- Seven Trumpets are blown on Yom Kippur.
- Those in tribulation are released.
- The earth is redeemed.

- God's people are restored to the inheritance.————————
- Christ establishes a Sabbath for the earth.————————

THE REASON FOR SEVEN SEALS

"And having turned I saw seven golden lamp-stands, and in the midst of the seven lampstands one like the Son of Man, clothed with a garment down to the feet and girded about the chest with a golden band.... He had in His right hand seven stars ... He laid His right hand on me, saying to me, 'Do not be afraid, I am the First and the Last.... The mystery of the seven stars which you saw in My right hand, and the seven golden lampstands: The seven stars are the angels of the seven churches, and the seven lampstands which you saw are the seven churches.' " - Revelation 1:12-13, 16-17, 20

Even though there were hundreds of churches in Asia Minor when John wrote the book of Revelation, only seven of them are mentioned. The leaders of these congregations are likened unto stars and their churches likened unto the seven branches of the menorah. I submit to you that what the branches of the menorah and stars have in common is "light." Light, as we know, illuminates and brings revelation to a dark situation. It seems that these seven churches are to serve as emblems of light; they are witnesses of Him who stands in the midst of the menorah – the First and Last.

This is important to understand because, in ancient times, when scrolls were sealed, often the seal was the signet ring of a witness impressed into clay or, later, wax. For that scroll to be read, the seven witnesses or their heirs must be present so that the legal requirements for breaking the seals are satisfied! The seven congregations in Asia are witnesses that He is Alpha and Omega (better tendered "Alef and Tav," the first and last in the Hebrew alphabet), the Beginning and the End.

As I mentioned earlier, for lands to be restored to the rightful owner sometimes required the assistance of a near kinsman, a Kinsman Redeemer. This is what the story of Ruth and Naomi is about. Naomi, the Jewess, had lost her inheritance due to the famine and other difficult circumstances. Upon the death of her husband and sons, she determines to return to Bethlehem, the land of her nativity. Her daughter-in-law, Ruth, is traveling with her.

Ruth is not Jewish, but is one who comes from among the Gentiles. Nevertheless, she determines to make Naomi's people her people and Naomi's God her God (Ruth 1:16). This devotion eventually leads to Naomi being reinstated to her inheritance through her near kinsman Boaz. Boaz is from Bethlehem, born of the tribe of Judah. In addition to marrying Ruth, he redeems all that belonged to Naomi's former husband, Elimelech, and her deceased sons (Ruth 4:9-10). In the end, this act of redemption gives birth to the house of David (Ruth 4:22). The point of all of this is to show that, like Naomi, Adam and all of his descendants lost the planet – our inheritance – to the Adversary. It took action in the form of the second Adam – Jesus, the kinsman Redeemer, born in Bethlehem of the tribe of Judah – to restore us back to our inheritance.

24

We should understand that being born again was just the start of that restoration. What happens with the opening of the seven-sealed scroll brings that restoration to fruition.

THE JUDGMENTS

Part of the process that brings everything into fruition is the necessity of judgment. When the seventh seal is loosed and the seventh trumpet sounded, seven vials are released upon the earth bringing judgment upon all of those who defied the God of Heaven. Yet, the Bible makes it clear that judgments upon the wicked are not the only judgments that are necessary to bring complete restoration.

In fact, it could be said that judgment is not necessarily bad – it just depends upon what side of the law you find yourself. If you are guilty, then there is a consequence. If you are innocent, then there is a reward. The Scripture seems to say that this is the type of judgment that will be dispensed during the Tribulation.

"The nations were angry, and Your wrath has come , and the time of the dead, that they should be judged, and that You should reward Your servants the prophets and the saints, and those who fear Your name, small and great, and should destroy those who destroy the earth." – Revelation 11:18

There is, apparently, another judgment after the Tribulation as well, meant to deal with those who died during the Tribulation.

"And many of those who sleep in the dust of the earth shall awake; some to everlasting life; some to shame and everlasting contempt." – Daniel 12:2

And finally, we see that there is to be what is called the Great White Throne Judgment.

"And I saw the dead, small and great, standing before God, and books were opened. And another book was opened, which is the Book of Life. And the dead were judged according to their works, by the things which were written in the books." - Revelation 20:12

At this final judgment, all of the unrighteous from Cain to the end of the Millennial Reign of Christ will be judged once and for all. This means that all of those who have been imprisoned in Hell, including fallen angels and Satan himself, will have to stand before God and give him an account. It is going to be an awesome and, yes, terrifying day.

And it all begins with the fact that books which had been sealed were opened. As they were opened, hidden truths – mysteries – were made known and God's Plan matured until it was finally completed. Now, if the books in heaven are going to be opened so that God's purposes may be accomplished, then I submit to you that His Book here on earth – the Bible – is also going to be opened. Things that we have never understood are going to be, for the first time, revealed. We can know what our God is doing because He wishes for us to know what He is doing.

Still, there is only One who is worthy to open to us

those mysteries contained in the Bible. Yet, it is He who, I believe, now says that the delay should be no longer (Revelation 10:6). I believe this book, "Breaking the Code of the Feasts," is one resource that will help unlock glorious mysteries of the future.

Chapter Two

GOD'S BEST
KEPT SECRET

"Nothing is hidden which will not be revealed, nor has anything been kept secret but that it should come to light." - Mark 4:22

It has been supposed by some that when Jesus uttered these words, His intent was to warn you and I to be careful what we say because anything spoken in secret would come to light. While it is absolutely true that we will be judged according to every idle word spoken, that is not the issue that Jesus was addressing in this particular passage. What he was telling us is, there is nothing that God has hidden that will not, when it is time, be revealed for all to see.

Consider the context of this statement. Jesus taught a parable about a sower scattering seed, which is the Word of God (Mark 4:14, Luke 8:11). In giving them this parable, Jesus acknowledged that He was telling them something that, if they grasped it, would unlock certain mysteries that had been kept since the foundation of the word (Mark 4:11, Matthew 13:34-35). In fact, He told them that this particular parable is unique because, if they do not understand the Parable of the Sower, then they will be unable to understand any of the other parables (Mark 4:13).

This is fascinating when you think about it. If one can comprehend this single parable, it will aid in unlocking any mystery contained within the others. This says to me that when we understand key principles in the Scripture, that principle will be the key to unlock other secret chambers contained within the Word of God. This also tells me that:

- God does have secrets.
- He keeps them secret until it is time for them to be revealed.
- He only reveals them to His people.
- When it is time, He will reveal them.

The prophet says:

"Surely the LORD God does nothing, unless He reveals His secret to His servants the prophets."
- Amos 3:7

There are other instances in Scripture where Jesus acknowledged the fact that God has secrets and that these secrets are intended to be revealed. Let us note just a few of these instances.

"For there is nothing covered, that will not be revealed and hidden that will not be known"
-Matthew 10:26

"You have hidden these things from the wise and prudent and revealed them to babes." - Matthew 11:25

"Therefore every scribe which instructed concerning the kingdom of heaven is like a householder who brings out of his treasure things new and old."
- Matthew 13:52

Everyone understands that Jesus came to save a lost world and thank God for it. Still, it is crucial to understand that He also came to teach us how to live after we are saved. In other words, it is important that we know what God wants us to do and to do that, we must understand what He is doing and how He is doing it. Therefore, Jesus came teaching us, not only about the existence of hidden things but, more importantly, what these hidden things are and what they mean.

FOUR LEVELS OF STUDY

Now, we must also understand that long before Jesus came, the notion that things were concealed in the Scripture - and that these things would be revealed - had been investigated, to say the least, by students of the Word throughout the centuries. Their perspective of this is found within an ancient concept referred to as פרדס *pardes*, meaning "garden" or "orchard." This methodology analyzes the

Scriptures, and specifically the Pentateuch (the five books of Moses), using four basic categories of interpretation. The four categories are listed here. (Notice the first letters of each word form the acronym P-R-D-S or *pardes*.)

- *Peshat* - The simple or literal meaning.
- *Remez* - The meaning hinted at in Scripture.
- *Derush* - The homiletic meaning of the text.
- *Sod* - The secret or concealed meaning.

The first category, *peshat* פשט, is the literal application; it means what it says. *Remez* רמז, the second category, is a "hint" or "inference." This means that we can learn truths from certain Scriptures that hint at something. In other words, certain things can be deduced from the text without actually being stated. However, according to the principle of *remez*, that it is not stated does not make it any less true.

The third category, *derush* דרוש, is what we detect from homiletics. That is to say, we learn a truth when we seek Biblical answers to Biblical questions. Most all of us are familiar with the biblical adage, "Precept upon precept..., line upon line, here a little, and there a little" (Isaiah 28:10). This passage teaches us that one must not make conclusions and to establish doctrine or belief based on one Scripture alone, and especially if it is taken out of context. Sound doctrinal interpretation is based on a concert of Scripture. This is what is meant by homiletics or *derush*.

Now we come to the fourth and, in my opinion, the most intriguing of these four categories of interpretation -

sod סוד, (pronounced sode) or "secret." *Sod* is to be understood as being "concealed" in the same way a foundation is concealed from view, and still we know that it is there. In fact, it is what holds up and stabilizes everything that is built upon it.

Where the Word of God is concerned, it is very possible that on many occasions, what is revealed on the surface of the text may be there to teach us about what is beneath the surface of the text. In other words, the principle of sod teaches us that God conceals messages within the Scripture. There is a hidden dimension of God's Word.

THE HIDDEN DIMENSION

Most Christians have never heard of the "inner dimension of the Torah," yet this is a very well-known concept in Judaism. It is so well- known that the revealing of this "inner dimension" is considered to be one of the signs of the Advent of the Messiah. According to rabbinic tradition, the Messiah would reveal new insights and would manifest the hidden mysteries of the Scriptures.

Consider that when we speak of rabbinic tradition, we are talking about conclusions that have been drawn by a group of people who had dedicated their entire lives to searching the Scriptures - they were no novices. Yet in their life-long search, many of these ancient rabbis were forced to acknowledge that there remained many passages whose true meaning still eluded them. They became convinced that there was a hidden "inner dimension" of the Scripture, which could only be revealed by the Messiah.

Not only did Jesus confirm the belief in an "inner

dimension" of Scripture, but as I stated earlier, He actually began to reveal what these hidden things were and how they were to be applied to our lives just as the Scripture said he would do.

"Give ear, O my people, to my law. Incline your ears to the words of my mouth. I will open my mouth in a parable; I will utter dark sayings of old, which we have heard and known, and our fathers have told us. We will not hide them from their children, telling to the generation to come the praises of the LORD."

- Psalm 78:1-4

If we take into account that Jews had long recognized this hidden dimension of Scripture, then it becomes clear that Jesus was meeting their Messianic expectations concerning this issue by confirming that there is such a thing as a concealed "inner dimension" of the Word of God. Not only that, but what becomes clear to me is this; the Messiah Jesus IS the inner, hidden dimension of the Word. The fact that so many people who should have recognized Him as Messiah but did not (not to mention the millions more who still have not) is evidence that our heavenly Father has and does conceal things within His Word.

Furthermore, this hidden dimension would have been handed down through rabbinical teaching to all those aspiring to understand more fully the Word of God. So then, when we ponder the reality that others besides Jesus were aware of these hidden treasures in Scripture, we should not be surprised to learn that Paul is chief among them.

PAUL AND MYSTERIES OF THE KINGDOM

Keep in mind that Paul was trained in Scripture at the feet of Rabban Gamaliel the Elder (Acts 22:3) and, consequently, would have been well acquainted with the concepts associated with the four levels of study - *peshat*, *remez*, *derush* and *sod*. It only seems logical that when he became a believer in Jesus the Messiah, he would have adapted the principles of what he already knew to what the Holy Spirit was revealing to him. Thus, Paul had a lot to say in his writings about these mysteries of the Kingdom. To the congregation at Ephesus he wrote:

"How that by revelation he made known to me the mystery; (as I have briefly written already, by which, when you read, you may understand my knowledge in the mystery of Christ), which in other ages was not made known to the sons of men, as it is now been revealed by the Spirit to His holy apostles and prophets ... And to make all see what is the fellowship of the mystery, which from the beginning of the ages has been hidden in God who created all things through Jesus Christ." - Ephesians 3:3-5, 9

To the congregation in Colosse, he wrote:

"I became a minister according to the stewardship from God which was given to me for you, to fulfill the word of God, the mystery which has been hidden from ages and from generations, but now has been revealed to His saints. To them God willed to make

known what are the riches of the glory of this mystery among the Gentiles; which is Christ in you, the hope of glory." - Colossians 1:25-27

To the Romans he wrote:

"Now to Him who is able to establish you according to my gospel and the preaching of Jesus Christ, according to the revelation of the mystery kept secret since the world began, but now has been made manifest, and by the prophetic Scriptures has been made known to all nations, according to the commandment of the everlasting God, for obedience to the faith."
- Romans 16:25-26

It becomes abundantly clear that Paul is well aware of the existence of these hidden elements within the Word of God and, so, he discusses them at length. Perhaps one of the more dramatic examples of this understanding is contained in a letter he addressed to the congregation at Corinth. In this letter he reiterated that key and essential truths had been hidden from the foundation of the world and, furthermore, that their disclosure before the appointed time would have been catastrophic to mankind.

"We speak wisdom among those who are mature, yet not the wisdom of this age, nor of the rulers of this age, who are coming to nothing. But we speak the wisdom of God in a mystery, the hidden wisdom which God ordained before the ages for our glory, which none of the rulers of this age knew; for had they known they

would not have crucified the Lord of glory. But as it is written: 'Eye has not seen nor ear heard, nor have entered into the heart of man the things which God has prepared for those who love Him.' But God has revealed them to us through His Spirit. For the Spirit searches all things, yes, the deep things of God."

- 1 Corinthians 2:6-10

These are the words of a person who was obviously moved upon by the Holy Spirit and who was initiated in the ancient traditions of Scriptural interpretation. So, when he refers to hidden wisdom that God foreordained, he can only be speaking of one thing - the "inner dimension" of Scripture and those things regarded as *sod* or "mysteries." In fact, the phrase "hidden wisdom" is translated from the Greek *apokrupto*, which means "to hide or conceal." The particular mystery that Paul addresses in this letter happens to be the greatest of all mysteries as far as Scripture is concerned - the death, burial and resurrection of the Messiah. Paul makes it clear that this mystery was deeply concealed that the princes of this world were totally unable to discern God's plan.

Why all the Scriptural cloak-and-dagger? Had they - the princes of this world - unraveled this mystery they would have never allowed Jesus to go to the cross. The ramifications of that scenario would be disastrous because, without the crucifixion, there is no resurrection and we would still be in our sin (1 Corinthians 15:17).

If by "princes" Paul is referring to earthly princes, i.e. the Jewish rulers, it is logical to conclude that they would not have killed the coming Anointed One. If Paul refers to spiritual princes, the rulers of the darkness of this world, they would certainly not have followed through with a plan that led to their own demise. Obviously, these principalities did not discern that the Messiah was to die and to rise again - that was a truth that had been hidden well.

Yes, God had hidden the Plan of Redemption from the very **foundation** (remember a foundation is hidden by what is built upon it) of Creation and why? There were those who, had they known, would have prevented it from coming to fruition. Reflect upon the fact that when God began to create the world, angels were present (Job 38:7). One of those angels, Lucifer, fell - we presume - after the creation of heaven and earth (Genesis 1).

Knowing all things, including that Satan would try to undermine God's plan for mankind, the heavenly Father had already developed a plan of redemption that would be hidden from "principalities and powers." Again, had they known His plan they would have attempted to stop it. As it turns out, their efforts to "stop" God's plan actually contributed to its success. Perhaps this is one of the reasons Scripture says:

"Having disarmed principalities and powers. He made a public spectacle of them, triumphing over them in it." - Colossians 2:15

And so, we understand that God hid the:

■ Virgin birth (Isaiah 7:14).
■ Mystery of the blood of Christ.

■ Death and resurrection of Christ (1 Cor. 2:8).

These mysteries were truths purposely kept concealed from the beginning of time, but at Messiah's coming, were revealed to those who had ears to hear. Likewise, we should understand that any truth that has remained a secret until these last days will also be revealed when it is time. I mean, do we really believe that **all** of God's mysteries have been unveiled? The prophet Daniel was told that certain things would remain a mystery until the end of days.

"But you, Daniel, shut up the words and seal the book until the time of the end. Many shall run to and fro, and knowledge shall increase." - Daniel 12:4

This passage teaches us two things. First of all, at the time of the end there would be mysteries that God's people did not understand. Nevertheless, at the time of the end, God would permit the understanding of these mysteries to be unveiled. How will these truths be finally revealed? According to Paul, comprehension of this "hidden wisdom" comes by the Holy Spirit as He opens our understanding of the Word of God.

IN THE MOUNT OF THE LORD

We understand that when God created the heavens and the earth, He did so completely. We also understand that, in every facet and era of human existence, God always knew just how to deal with mankind. Again, the Lamb was "slain from the foundation of the world." (Revelation 13:8). Though He always knew these things, mankind did not always know. So then, through the millennia, God has systematically revealed these hidden truths, and in particular, how He intended to redeem mankind; the mystery of mysteries.

Consider that when mankind fell, God immediately began to reveal that a Redeemer would one day save the sons of men. It was in the Garden that He promised the Seed of the Woman would come and bruise the head of the serpent (Genesis 3:15). After that prophecy, there were only vague hints at the Promised One. That changed, however, when God found a friend in a man He called Abraham.

When Abraham was already an old man, he was told that he would have a son - a promised son. Through this promised one, Abraham would become the father of many nations. After that son, Isaac, was born and had matured into a lad, Abraham was told to take him to the mountains of Moriah and there offer him as a burnt offering.

"Now it came to pass after these things that God tested Abraham, and said to him, 'Abraham!' And he said, 'Here I am.' Then He said, 'Take now your son, your only son Isaac, whom you love, and go to the land of Moriah, and offer him there as a burnt offering on one of the mountains of which I shall tell you.' So Abraham rose early in the morning and . . . went to the place of which God had told him. Then on the third day Abraham lifted his eyes and saw the place afar off . . . so Abraham took the wood of the burnt offering and laid it on Isaac his son; and he took the fire in his hand, and a

knife, and the two of them went together. But Isaac spoke to Abraham his father and said, 'My father!' And he said, 'Here I am, my son.' Then he said, 'Look, the fire and the wood, but where is the lamb for a burnt offering?' And Abraham said, 'My son, God will provide for Himself the lamb for a burnt offering.' So the two of them went together. Then they came to the place of which God had told him." - Genesis 22:1-4, 6-9

First notice that God told Abraham to take his **only** son, Isaac. Why did He say "only son" when, in fact, Abraham had another son called Ishmael? It is because God considered Isaac to be the promised "seed" through which the covenant He made with Abraham would be fulfilled.

"**But God said to Abraham, 'Do not let it be displeasing in your sight because of the lad or because of your bondwoman. Whatever Sarah has said to you, listen to her voice, for in Isaac your seed shall be called.'**"
- Genesis 21:12

The **promised son** was to become a burnt offering. In fact, when God told Abraham to "offer him there as a burnt offering," the Hebrew literally says to "**lift him up**" upon the altar as a burnt offering (based upon the Hebrew root עלה *alah* from which the word עלה *olah* "burnt offering" is derived). Notice also that Isaac is the one who carried the wood. The Hebrew text literally says he carried a "tree" (from the Hebrew word עץ *etz*) and seeing that it was "laid" upon him, the inference is that it was laid upon his back. So, the promised son walked to the top of the mountain with a tree upon his back.

Now consider the place these events occurred. Abraham was directed to travel to the "land of Moriah." Today this area is known as Jerusalem and, specifically, the Temple Mount. This is the same area where, years after this event, Abraham's grandson Jacob saw a vision of angels ascending into and descending from heaven upon a staircase. This vision caused that startled Jacob to declare:

"This is none other than the house of God, and this is the gate of heaven." - Genesis 28:17

As father and son neared the landscape that would one day include the House of God - a place where countless offerings would be made - the Bible says that Abraham saw "the place afar off" on the "third day" (Genesis 22:4). The fact that he saw this place on the "third day" is interesting enough, but there is more here than meets the eye when we read the text in English. So, let us look a this phrase in Hebrew. The Hebrew word translated as "the place" is המקום *ha makom*. What makes this so interesting is, not only is *ha makom* understood to be "the place," but is also considered to be a name for God because He is in every place.

"If I ascend into heaven, You are there. If I make my bed in hell, behold, You are there." - Psalm 139:8

In any place you can imagine, God is already there; He is Omnipresent, thus He is "The Place." So, not only did Abraham "see" the place where the Temple would one day stand, but using this rabbinical interpretation of *Ha makom* as "the LORD," on the third day, he "saw the LORD afar off" (Genesis 22:4).

The word translated as "afar off" is מרחק *merchok*. It stems from the word רחק *rachak*, which means "remote (in space or time)" or "a great while to come." This interpretation hints at the idea that Abraham probably saw into the future. In fact, Jewish tradition believes that Abraham had a vision of a future event, hinted at by the word *merchok*. Evidently, whatever it was he saw had something to do with the LORD. Furthermore, his vision of the future convinced Abraham that, on Mount Moriah, the LORD would be seen.

It seems clear to me that he saw into the future and observed that God would "see (to) Himself a lamb." This literal interpretation points to the fact that God would see to it Himself; in other words, He would become **the** Lamb (the Hebrew text renders it השה *ha seh* - *ha* being the definite article) not merely provide a lamb. Apparently, Abraham saw the LORD, the Lamb of God, being executed near "the place" where he was taking Isaac - Mount Moriah - 2000 years before it actually happened! This is why he called the place "The LORD will Provide," or more properly *Yahweh Yireh* (Genesis 22:14).

"And Abraham lifted up his eyes, and looked, and behold behind him a ram caught in a thicket by his horns: and Abraham went and took the ram, and offered him up for a burnt offering in the stead of his son. And Abraham called the name of that place Jehovah-jireh: as it is said to this day, In the mount of the Lord it shall be seen." - Genesis 22:13-14 (KJV)

When Abraham discovers a ram in the thicket, the Hebrew text uses the word, איל *ayil* - **a ram**. In other words, the ram in the thicket became the substitute sacrifice for Isaac, but was obviously not "the lamb" spoken of by Abraham. Perhaps that is precisely why Abraham declares that, "in the mount of the Lord IT shall be seen" (Genesis 22:14). The question is what is the "it"? I believe that the name Abraham gave the place, *Yahweh Yireh*, gives us the answer. Understood literally, *Yahweh Yireh* is "Yahweh, He will see (to it)," and so it could be understood as "in the mount, Yahweh shall be seen!"

Jesus said, "Your father Abraham rejoiced to see my day: and he saw it, and was glad . . . Most assuredly I say to you, before Abraham was, I am" (John 8:56). It seems likely that Abraham was permitted to see into the future and understand that God Himself would be the Lamb and would suffer in the place of all mankind - and he saw it on the third day no less. Consider the following.

- Abraham took "his only son."
- Isaac is the Promised Seed.
- Isaac laid the wood (tree) on his back.
- Abraham said, "God will provide himself a lamb."
- A ram, not a lamb, was caught in the thicket.
- God provided a substitute offering.

In the time of Abraham, God announced in dramatic fashion how He intended to redeem mankind - God would become flesh and die on his behalf. Yet, keep this in mind: the Lamb was slain from the foundation of the world. That is what He had always intended. Furthermore, even though God made this very clear through the Scripture, until the Messiah was resurrected from the dead, no one understood it - except Abraham.

And thus this example clearly reveals the "inner dimension" of the Scripture, the prophetic layers found within the Sacred Text and the progressive revelation of God's Word.

Chapter Three

THE PROGRESSION
OF REVELATION

In the previous chapter I mentioned the fact that, throughout history, God has systematically revealed hidden truths, and in particular, how He intended to redeem mankind. It should also be noted that He didn't reveal everything all at one time and when He did grant revelation of certain things, it was sometimes cloaked in symbolism. The Plan of Redemption is just such an example. Still, it needs to be said again; had the princes of this world been able to decipher God's true intent, they would have attempted to foil it - thus, secrecy. I think it would be fair to say that God often hides things in plain sight and the greatest example of this is Messiah's birth, death, burial and resurrection.

But let us move on from there and broaden our discussion to examine how God allows revelation of **all** things to proceed in this manner. That means God reveals His intents and purposes in progression, and not "everything, all at once."

THE PLACE OF REDEMPTION

Jewish tradition has it that Jerusalem was the place where God stood when He created earth. Specifically, a particular area of the present-day Temple Mount marks the spot where God "hovered" as the world came into existence. That spot is called אבן שתיה *even shetiyah* - the "foundation stone." The Talmud records this as being the place where:

- God stood to create the rest of the world.
- Abraham bound Isaac as a burnt offering.
- Jacob rested his head and saw the vision.
- God took the stones to carve the first tablets of the Law.
- The Ark of the Covenant eventually rested.
- The blood of Yom Kippur was sprinkled.

Of course, this "foundation stone" is located on what is now the most disputed piece of land in all of the world - the Temple Mount in Jerusalem. In other words this place is special, to say the least, and becomes indelibly linked to God's plan in dealing with the redemption of man. If the Blood of the Messiah is the ink by which God's redemptive plan was penned, then Jerusalem is the scroll upon which it was written.

The importance of Jerusalem is this: it marks The Place God chose to commune with mankind. In the begin-

ning, God communed with man in the "midst of the garden." Before he fell, Adam clearly functioned in the role of
a priest. He would meet with God there in what was, no
doubt, a Most Holy Place. By the way, there is overwhelming evidence to support the notion that what is now called
the Temple Mount was once the center of the Garden of
Eden.

Twenty-five hundred years after Adam, Moses was
called up to the top of Mt. Sinai and there saw the heavenly Temple. From the pattern that he was shown in the
mount, he built the tabernacle (Hebrews 8:5). In the midst
of that Tabernacle was a chamber where God scheduled a
meeting with the appointed High Priest once a year on the
Day of Atonement. It is said that the Day of Atonement was
the only day that Satan was not permitted to rail accusations
at Israel. Why? Because God was meeting with His people.
Perhaps this is one of the reasons Satan hates Israel so desperately; the tent of the meeting on earth was patterned after
what existed in heaven - the place Satan was expelled from
(Luke 10:18).

Here is what I want you to see: the revelation of the
Tabernacle and what it was based upon - what man had
experienced in the Garden and what Moses saw in the
mountain - **gave God access to man on Earth**.

The next step on this revelation came to David three
thousand years after Adam and five hundred years after
Moses. It was permitted for David, and through him
mankind, to see the importance of Jerusalem and the
Temple that would adorn her.

After David took the stronghold of Zion, he moved
the capital of his kingdom from Hebron (where Abraham

was buried) to the city of Jerusalem; a city of which it is written:

"Beautiful in elevation; the joy of the whole earth is Mount Zion on the sides of the north, the city of the great King." - Psalm 48:2

Provoked by the desire to see a house built in Jerusalem for his God, David was given a vision of the Temple. However, even though he was given the plans for the Temple, he was not permitted to build it. That honor was given to his son Solomon.

"You shall not build Me a house to dwell in...And it shall be, when your days are fulfilled,...that I will set up your seed after you, who will be of your sons, and I will establish his kingdom. He shall build me a house, and I will establish his throne forever. I will be his Father, and he shall be My son, ... and I will establish him in My house and in My kingdom forever, and his throne shall be established forever."
- 1 Chronicles 17:4, 11-14

As we know, Solomon did indeed build the Temple, which history records as being a structure of untold wealth and indescribable beauty. Still, the most important thing to understand about the First Temple was that it was the place Man had the privilege, indeed the duty, of meeting with God here on Earth. Let me remind you that, in all probability, it was the same place where Adam had communed with God and where Abraham found a ram and saw the Lamb!

WHERE HEAVEN AND EARTH MEET

In the above Scripture, it is presumed that the son of David that God referred to - the one whose throne was to be established forever - was Solomon. I believe that on one level - the literal level of interpretation - that is who it refers to. Yet, recall that Scripture is to be understood on four basic levels of interpretation - *peshat*, *remez*, *derush*, and *sod*. That being said, who should we interpret David's son to be if we view this Scripture on the level of *sod*, the hidden dimension? Consider the following Scriptures.

"When Jesus departed from there, two blind men followed Him, crying out and saying 'Son of David, have mercy on us!' " - Matthew 9:27

"And all the multitudes were amazed and said, 'Could this be the Son of David?' " - Matthew 12:23

"And behold, a woman of Canaan came from that region and cried out to Him, saying, 'Have mercy on me, O Lord, Son of David!' " - Matthew 15:22

"Then the multitudes who went before and those who followed cried out, saying, 'Hosanna to the Son of David! Blessed is He who comes in the name of the LORD.' " - Matthew 21:9

Scripture declares that it is Jesus Christ, the Son of David who will rule and reign forever. It is His throne that has been eternally established by God.

"The kingdoms of this world have become the kingdoms of our Lord and of His Christ, and he shall reign forever and ever." - Revelation 11:15

Every aspect of His life and ministry - the virgin birth, that His blood would save people from their sins, etc. - was revealed in Scripture and yet, for the most part, hidden from everyone until it was accomplished. When He did accomplish God's redemptive Plan, the crowning moment - the Resurrection - provided yet another revelation.

Where the Tabernacle had given God access to Man and the Temple had given Man access to God, the Resurrection brought heaven and earth together in every human heart that believed. Paul said:

"Do you not know that your body is the temple of the Holy Spirit who is in you, whom you have from God, and you are not your own? For you were bought at a price, therefore glorify God in your body and in your spirit, which are God's." - 1 Corinthians 6:19

Scripture also promises that, because of the work of the Messiah, God and Man will meet together eternally in the New Jerusalem, fulfilling the "restoration of all things" (Acts 3:21). Thus, all the revelation that had previously been unveiled was intended to bring man to this point of understanding - that in the end, man would once again commune with God and God with man just as it had been in the beginning.

A LIGHT UNTO THE GENTILES

Another truth that was exposed by the resurrection of the Messiah was that God intended to do a work among Jew AND Gentile. Initially, this was a bit difficult even for those Jews who were believers in Jesus as Messiah to come to grips with. In the end, the LORD used a converted tormentor of those early believers and sent him to the Gentiles to reveal something that had been hidden from the very beginning. The Apostle Paul related that:

"When it pleased God, who separated me from my mother's womb and called me through His grace, to reveal His Son in me, that I might preach Him among the Gentiles, I did not immediately confer with flesh and blood, nor did I go up to Jerusalem to those who were apostles before me; but I went to Arabia, and returned again to Damascus." - Galatians 1:15-17

It should be noted that Mount Sinai is in Arabia (Galatians 4:25) and was the place where God revealed great and marvelous things to Israel through Moses. It seems likely that Paul traveled to Sinai and learned great and mysterious things concerning the "other flock" that Jesus had come to suffer and die for. Remember, Jesus had said:

"Other sheep I have which are not of this fold; them also I must bring, and they will hear My voice, and there will be one flock and one shepherd." - John 10:16

It was primarily Paul who made known the mystery concerning the Gentiles; that is, that they too were to come into the knowledge of the one true God and His Messiah. He understood that Christ was the promised "light to the Gentiles" (Isaiah 49:6, 60:3). Consequently, he also emphasized that this was a mystery that had been hidden since the foundation of the world!

"When you read, you may understand my knowledge in the mystery of Christ , which in other ages was not made known to the sons of men, as it has now been revealed by the Spirit to His holy apostles and prophets: that the gentiles should be fellow heirs, of the same body and partakers of his promise in Christ through the gospel of which I became a minister according to the gift of the grace of God given to me by the effective working of His power. To me, who am less than the least of all the saints, this grace was given, that I should preach among the Gentiles the unsearchable riches of Christ, and to make all see what is the fellowship of the mystery, which from the beginning of the ages has been hidden in God who created all things through Jesus Christ." - Ephesians 3:4-9

Paul also, more than any other, emphasizes the resurrection of all believers in the last days.

"Behold, I tell you a mystery. We shall not all sleep, but we shall all be changed - in a moment, in the twinkling of an eye, at the last trumpet. For the trumpet will sound, and the dead will be raised incorruptible,

and we shall be changed." - 1 Corinthians 15:51-52

"For if we believe that Jesus died and rose again, even so God will bring with Him those who sleep in Jesus. For this we say to you by the word of the Lord, that we who are alive and remain until the coming of the Lord will by no means precede whose who are asleep. For the Lord Himself will descend from heaven with a shout, with the voice of an archangel, and with the trumpet of God. And the dead in Christ will rise first. Then we who are alive and remain shall be caught up together with them in the clouds to meet the Lord in the air. And thus we shall always be with the Lord."
- 1 Thessalonians 4:14-17

So, what began with a tabernacle in the wilderness - a place where God would meet with man - ends with the revelation that God would, once again, come down to meet with man, but this time in the air! And this time, not only would He come for those who are referred to as Israel, but also those who were among the Gentiles who had been grafted into and become one with His people Israel.

Through this progressive revelation, we see that there are prophetic layers in the Scripture which reveal future events! To understand the truths hidden in these layers, study is required. Without a doubt, the time that Paul spent in Arabia was filled with study of the Scripture. Study alone, however, is not the answer. True revelation comes through spending time with the Father in prayer and seeking understanding of what we study. I can easily imagine that being in Sinai also prompted Paul to seek God's face for answers to many of the questions he had about the Scripture.

Hence, when searching the Word of God for answers, I recommend this methodology:

- Read the text to understand the literal and historical account.
- Compare Scripture with more Scripture.
- Do word studies to understand the original meaning.
- Analyze the prophetic layers in the Scripture.
- Seek the face of God.

LEARNING FROM PICTURES

"That which has been is what will be; that which is done is what will be done, and there is nothing new under the sun." - Ecclesiastes 1:9

As we study these prophetic layers, it should be noted that many times these layers are hidden in types and shadows - pictures. From the very beginning God has given us pictures with the Word that are to teach us of even greater principles.

At the very beginning of Creation, He made the heavenly luminaries - the sun, moon and stars - for days and years, for seasons and for **signs** (Genesis 1:14). In other words, these signs serve to point to something greater. The moon, for instance is crucial in determining time from a biblical perspective, because new moons, sabbaths and feast times are dependent on the lunar cycle. These feasts, sabbaths, and new moons, in turn are critical in understanding how God works in the earth. They are pictures that teach of spiritual principles as well as shedding light on things to come.

"Let no one judge you in food or in drink, or regarding a festival or a new moon or sabbath, which are a shadow of things to come, but the substance is of Christ." - Colossians 2:16-17

The seven feasts of Israel, the sabbaths and other principles found in the teachings of Moses are understood to be "shadows of things to come." They point us to things God wishes for us to understand. Yet, even though they teach us of other things - they are shadows - the one casting the shadow is Christ Himself. In other words, don't dismiss as obsolete that which casts the shadow.

The "hidden dimension" of Scripture is also contained in the narratives provided in the Bible. As we read in Ecclesiastes 1 and as we have observed in the Scripture, the past indeed reveals the future. The picture can be found in a person's life story, a dramatic event, or anything designed to represent something else. As we have already seen, Genesis 22 and the binding of Isaac is a detailed picture of the crucifixion of Christ. There are dozen of other examples that point to Christ and His suffering. Here are just a couple notable examples.

■ Numbers 19 and the Red Heifer are a picture of the crucifixion of Christ.

- Exodus 12 and the Passover Lamb contain a picture of the power of Christ's blood.
- The brass serpent on the pole is a preview of Christ on the cross.

NEVER BEFORE ITS TIME

Wherever and however these hidden things are embedded in Scripture, the pictures they paint for us are never understood until it is time for them to be revealed. That means that some things are just now coming to light. Recall what Daniel was told.

"But you Daniel, shut up the words and seal the book until the time of the end. Many shall run to and fro, and knowledge shall increase" - Daniel 12:4

This Scripture makes it clear that some mysteries are sealed until the time of the end and those of us living in that time should expect that these hidden things are becoming evident.

One example that comes to mind is what is now known as the "Bible Codes." Back in the late 1980s, I was alerted to this phenomena while on a trip to Israel. Upon early investigation it became clear that there was indeed something to this. In short, these codes are based on Equidistant Letter Sequences (ELS). When proper methodology is applied, it has been found that encoded messages, notable personalities and historic events can be found hidden in the Hebrew text, particularly the five books of Moses

- the Torah.

Even though some rabbis have known about this phenomena for decades, perhaps centuries, most of them did not realize the extent of this biblical peculiarity. It proves beyond doubt, at least as far as I am concerned, that the Bible is the Word of God, that it predicts events before they happen and God is desperately trying to reach this last day generation.

Why has God waited until now to reveal things such as this? I believe it is because some things would not have been understood or even possible until this generation. Without the use of computers, for instance, Bible Codes would be almost impossible to validate as legitimate. Therefore, I will give you for fundamental reasons why I believe God has waited until now to reveal certain mysteries.

- Population
- Education
- Transportation
- Communication

It has been suggested that in Jesus' time the earth was populated with about 200 million people. Today there are over 300 million in the United States alone and nearly seven billion people globally. This means that, in the present age, more people can be reached with the Gospel than at any other time in history. We can potentially reach more people in this generation than all the people who have ever lived in previous generations combined.

In days gone by, relatively few people were educated to the degree that they are now. The limits on education most likely limited biblical understanding as well. That is not to say that there has been no understanding, it is to say that, if a person could not read the Scripture for himself, he was dependent on someone else - in most cases clergy - to teach him the Scripture. In our time more people have achieved some level of higher education, so then, the potential for greater understanding of the Scriptures exists, perhaps as never before.

Not only do we have more people and more educated people at that, but they are traveling everywhere taking their knowledge with them. For centuries people walked, rode animals or sailed upon the water. Then came carriages, trains and steamships. The 20th century saw the advent of the airplane and the automobile. In our day, planes travel at supersonic speeds while trains and cars, though slower, cover ground at incredible speeds as well. This phenomenal increase in transportation methods and their speed has caused the world to shrink. The result has been that the transfer of ideas and information is extensive and quick. God has used this increase of knowledge - "many shall run to and fro" - to spread His Word.

Prior to Genesis 11 and the Tower of Babel, all mankind spoke one language. Because they had determined to come together in defiance of God, He went down, confused their languages and scattered mankind around the earth. When the Scripture was first given to mankind it was in the Hebrew tongue. Eventually it was translated into Greek, then Latin and now most every language. Perhaps most prominent among them is English. In our lifetime, we have seen English become the universal language, making it possible to communicate the Scripture with almost every nationality in one language.

Technological advancements in communication have helped in this venture - DVDs, computers and, of course the Internet. Today, someone in the United States can communicate with someone on the other side of the world in real time or, through mass media, without ever meeting the person and can speak to them as many times as that person wishes to listen to a CD or watch a DVD.

Now that we have briefly discussed why I think God has waited until now to reveal certain things, let us now look at a few examples of these mysteries that He has reserved for the end of the age.

PROPHECIES RESERVED FOR THE END

Centuries ago before the discovery of flight, Sir Isaac Newton predicted that the outcasts of Israel would return to their ancient homeland by actually flying there. He based that prediction upon the following prophecy.

"But they shall fly down upon the shoulder of the Philistines toward the west. Together they shall plunder the people of the east: They shall lay their hand on Edom and Moab; and the people of Ammon shall obey them" - Isaiah 11:14

Of course, people scoffed at Newton's prediction, but as we know, many Jews have returned to the land of Israel by flying into Ben Gurion Airport just outside of Tel

Aviv. Interestingly, when you look at an older map of Israel - one showing ancient boundaries - you will discover that where the Ben Gurion Airport now sits would be on the upper part of ancient Philistia. In other words, upon their shoulder just as the prophecy predicted. The point is, until now, that prophecy was a mystery and would not have been understood as a literal prophecy. Now that men travel by aircraft everyday, the mystery - or at least part of it - has been cleared up. Let us look at a similar prophecy.

"Behold, he is coming with clouds, and every eye will see him, even they who pierced him: and all the tribes of the earth will mourn because of him. Even so, Amen." - Revelation 1:7

To truly understand this prophecy, we must first of all discuss the meaning of "with clouds."

We know about the prophecy Paul spoke of where those of us who are still alive and all the dead in Christ are to meet Him in the clouds. It is interesting to note that the Greek text does not include the definite article, meaning the text literally says that we who are alive will be:

"Caught up together with them in clouds to meet the Lord in the air" - 1 Thessalonians 4:17

Jesus said that He would return in **a cloud** with power (Luke 21:27). It was a **single cloud** that received Him out of sight as He ascended into heaven (Acts 1:9). Now consider that the writer of Hebrews recorded that we are surrounded by a great "cloud of witnesses" (Hebrew

12:1). The key to understanding Paul's prophecy is to know that the Greek root word translated as "cloud" in Hebrews 12:1 (*nephos*) is the same one used in Luke 21, in Acts 1 and in 1 Thessalonians 4. In other words, it is very likely that the clouds in all these passages are not the collection of moisture vapors that gather in the sky above us.

The writer of Hebrews uses *nephos* or "cloud" to paint a picture of a large group gathered in a stadium to watch the athletes down on the field. This Greek word is used in classical Greek to speak of a "cloud" or gathering of foot soldiers!

Apparently then, when Jesus was ascending into heaven, the cloud that received Him were all of those who had been raised from the dead with Him (Matthew 27:52-53). That great cloud of witnesses mentioned in Hebrews has to be those who have gone into the presence of the Lord (2 Corinthians 5:8). When He returns as King of kings and Lord of lords, the cloud He comes with is when the family of God in HEAVEN and in EARTH meet together as one!

Now getting back to the prophecy in Revelation 1, it says He is "coming with clouds." Hopefully, we understand that part of it much better now. Still, there is something else here that needs to be discussed and that is that "every eye" shall see Him. When John wrote this prophecy, that would have been utterly impossible. However, in our day it is very possible. With the technology that exists in our generation, you and I can watch something going on in Israel in real time. It is likely that, at the end of the Great Tribulation, people will be watching television to see the latest on the great war developing in Israel. All of a sudden something is going to appear in the heavens - the Son of

Man coming to destroy all the enemies gathered against His people! Every eye shall see Him!

"He causes all, both small and great, rich and poor, free and slave, to receive a mark on their right hand or on their foreheads." - Revelation 13:16

Again, when John wrote these words down, it would have been nearly impossible for everyone in his generation to be marked in this manner. Yet today we can imagine how someone with as much power as the Antichrist will possess could use today's (not to mention tomorrow's) technology to bring everyone under his complete control. In our world one little magnetic strip on the back of a card can contain as much information as can be accumulated in a lifetime.

Every day we advance further toward a cashless society where all of our critical information is amassed and maintained in a digital format. Furthermore, the technology now exists for this information to be imbedded into your skin eliminating the need to carry cards that might be stolen. I believe this technology has been developed, primarily, for noble purposes. Still, one day a man will arise who will use this technology for evil. He will seek to control the world's markets making it impossible for people to function in any way, unless they submit to his control.

"And that no one may buy or sell, except one who has the mark, or the name of the beast, or the number of his name." - Revelation 13:17

We live in a day in which all are known by some type of number whether it be a social security number, a bank account number, a street address and so on. Without these numbers we could not exist in today's society and so we see how this prophecy could come to pass in our day and time.

"And he cried with a loud cry to him who had the sharp sickle, saying 'Thrust in your sharp sickle and gather the clusters of the vine of the earth, for her grapes are fully ripe.' So the angel thrust his sickle the earth and gathered the vine of the earth, and threw it into the great winepress of the wrath of God. And the winepress was trampled outside the city, and blood came out of the winepress, up to the horses' bridles, for one thousand six hundred furlongs."
- Revelation 14:18-20

This is one of those prophecies that not only was a great mystery in ancient times, but whose understanding remains elusive even in our day. First of all, who uses horses in modern warfare? Second, does it really mean that the blood will literally be this deep? Lastly, if this is a description of what happens during the battle of Armageddon (which is an enormous valley) as many suppose, why is a city mentioned and what city is it? Let us deal with where this battle takes place first.

"And I saw three unclean spirits like frogs coming out of the mouth of the dragon, out of the mouth of the beast , and out of the mouth of the false prophet. For

they are spirits of demons, performing signs, which go out to the kings of the earth and of the whole world, to gather them to the battle of that great day of God Almighty. . . . And they gathered them together to the place called in Hebrew, Armageddon."

- Revelation 16:13-14, 16

Notice that the "kings of the earth" gathered or assembled in the placed called Armageddon. It does **not** say that the battle takes place there although that has been the conclusion many have come to. However, the Scripture makes it clear that the climactic "battle of that great day of God Almighty" will be Jerusalem!

"I will also gather all nations, and bring them down to the Valley of Jehoshaphat and I will enter into judgement with them there on account of My people, My heritage Israel, whom they have scattered among the nations . . . Let the nations be wakened, and come up to the valley of Jehoshaphat, for there I will sit to judge all the surrounding nations. Put in the sickle, for the harvest is ripe, come, go down, for the winepress is full, the vats overflow - for their wickedness is great."

- Joel 3:2, 12-13

"When the Son of Man comes in His glory, and all the holy angels with Him, then He will sit on the throne of His glory. All the nations will be gathered before Him, and He will separate them one from another, as a shepherd divides his sheep from the goats."

- Matthew 25:31-32

Notice that, according to Joel, the nations who assemble at Armageddon march to Jerusalem and gather in the "valley of Jehoshaphat." Notice, too, that the "winepress is full," so the "sickle" is thrust in just as described in Revelation 14. These nations are gathered in the Valley of Jehoshaphat as Christ returns to take His throne. Since He returns to the Mt. of Olives, which faces Jerusalem on the east (Zechariah 14:4), the evidence suggests that the armies of the nations will most likely be gathered in the Kidron valley, which is just "outside the city." There they will be trampled down in the winepress of God's wrath. Others have made note of the fact that the decisive battle is in Jerusalem, not Armageddon.

"Bengel thinks the valley of Kidron, between Jerusalem and the mount of Olives, is meant, its torrent being about to be discoloured with blood for 1,600 furlongs. This accords with Joel's prophecy, that the valley of Jehoshaphat is to be the scene of overthrow of the anti-Christian foes."
-Jamieson, Fausset and Brown Commentary

The Kidron, or the valley of Jehoshaphat, is very deep and narrow. It is unlikely that tanks and armored personnel carriers could maneuver efficiently in this setting. In other words, it seems the perfect place for armies that still utilize horse flesh to use them. You have to keep in mind that these same nations would have witnessed the total annihilation of Gog's multitudinous armies and all of his sophisticated equipment (Ezekiel 38 & 39). Maybe their destruction came about through the use of an electromagnetic pulse. If the armies that march on Jerusalem suspect something like that might be used on them, then horses would prove to be valuable. Whatever the reason, it seems these armies assembled in the valley, or at least a portion of them, are on horseback.

Now, I must point out that some have assumed that the description of blood "up to the horses' bridles" is mere hyperbole. For example, one famous commentator said of this great pool of blood:

"A hyperbolical expression to denote a great effusion of blood. The Jews said, 'When Hadrian besieged the city called Bitter, he killed so many that the horses waded in blood up to their mouths.' The same kind of hyperbole with that above."

- Adam Clarke's Commentary

Perhaps, but it should also be noted that some countries still use horses, Afghanistan, Pakistan, Iran and Iraq among them. Furthermore, people have often been proven wrong when they were hesitant to take the Bible literally. So then, is it possible that this is to be interpreted literally? Is it not possible that, when Christ returns and destroys all those assembled against Jerusalem, their bodies will be piled as high as the horses' bridle? This is still a mystery but is becoming clearer in our day.

"Standing at a distance for fear of her torment saying, 'Alas, alas that great city Babylon, that mighty city! For in one hour your judgment has come.' "

- Revelation 18:10

According to history, the city of Rome was all but completely destroyed with fire while, according to legend, the Emperor Nero danced and made merry as the music played on. History records that Rome's destruction didn't happen overnight, or even in a day and a night, but that it took several days.

Throughout history, Jerusalem has been sacked and burned multiple times. Each time it was destroyed it took days, even weeks, for the end to come. Nevertheless here is a prophecy, written in a time when both of these cities experienced destruction by fire, that declares the great city of "Babylon" will be destroyed in just **one hour**!

When John recorded this mystery, there was no way, at least in human terms, that a great city such as he saw could be destroyed in one hour. This is another one of those mysteries that has been reserved for our time. Because, as we all know, only in the 20th century has it become possible to destroy an entire city in one hour.

The Scripture says that this great city will be "utterly burned with fire" in one day (Revelation 18:9) and that the people of the earth will "weep and lament for her when they see the smoke of her burning" (Revelation 18:9). People on land and on sea, for fear of falling victim to whatever destroyed her, remain afar off and watch her burn (Revelation 18:10, 17).

The only thing known to man that could accomplish this destruction in such a brief time is a non-conventional explosive device - a nuclear explosion of some type, which leads to the next mystery reserved for the end time.

"And this shall be the plague with which the

LORD will strike all people who fought against Jerusalem; their flesh shall dissolve while they stand on their feet; their eyes shall dissolve in their sockets, and their tongues shall dissolve in their mouths"
- Zechariah 14:12

Flesh consumed, eyes melted away in their sockets, tongues dissolved in their mouths before their bodies hit the ground - sounds similar to the effects of the intense and immediate heat generated by a nuclear explosion. Because their bodies *do* hit the ground - inferring they are not consumed - has led some to think that a neutron bomb might be used. Whatever it might be, the point is, this is another mystery that has been reserved for the end of days.

How could Zechariah or anyone alive during his day have imagined anything that destructive short of what would happen to a human being at the appearance of the LORD Himself? That being said, this destruction *is* what occurs to them who fight against Jerusalem; those same nations who gather in the valley of Jehoshaphat (Kidron). Interestingly, the Scripture does warn those who oppose Him that they will be destroyed "with the brightness of His coming" (2 Thessalonians 2:8).

I want to look at one more unusual prediction that could not have been understood until the present time and that has to do with, of all things, chariots in the battle.

"For the LORD will restore the excellence of Jacob like the excellence of Israel, for the emptiers have emptied them out and ruined their vine branches. The shields of his mighty men are made red . . . The chariots

come with flaming torches in the day of his preparation
. . . The chariots rage in the streets, they jostle one
another in the broad roads: they seem like torches, they
run like lightning." - Nahum 2:2-4

"With a noise like chariots over mountaintops
they leap, like the noise of a flaming fire that devours
the stubble, like a strong people set in battle array."
- Joel 2:5

What makes these prophecies so interesting is that
they are mysteries reserved for this day, but ironically,
would have been understood to a degree in the day they
were written. In other words, Nahum and Joel knew full-
well what a chariot was. Nevertheless, we know that chariots are no longer used in warfare and haven't been for centuries - or have they?

Years ago, I remember being in Israel and being
introduced to the newest tank in the Israeli arsenal. Its name
was (and is) the *Merkavah*. What shocked me was when I
found out what the Hebrew word *merkavah* means - "chariot"! In fact, that is the exact word Joel uses in his prophecy with the exception that it is in the feminine form
merkavot.

Nahum describes them as moving fast through wide
open places with fire spewing from their torches. Could this
be a description of the modern Israeli "chariot," the tank
called *Merkavah*?

All of the prophecies we have examined are mysteries that can only be cleared up by the passage of time. In
other words, revelation of God's Word is progressive. That

we are living in the end of the age must mean that most of the mysteries are about to be revealed and understood; that should excite you - it certainly excites me!

Now, let us focus on some Scriptures that many think have provided all the "nuggets" they had to offer. As you will see, these Scriptures contain a hidden vein so rich that it could only be appreciated in these last days.

Chapter Four

THE EXODUS CODE

"Moreover brethren, I do not want you to be unaware that all our fathers were under the cloud, all passed through the sea, all were baptized into Moses in the cloud and in the sea . . . Now all these things happened to them as examples, and they were written for our admonition, upon whom the ends of the ages have come." - 1 Corinthians 10:1-2, 11

Through Moses, God established and ordained for all time seven *moedim* ("appointed times") that we typically refer to as the seven feasts of Israel. These seven feasts are notably featured on God's calendar and were fixed in accordance with cycles already inherent in nature - rain cycles and harvest cycles. In the spring and fall comes the rains - the former and the latter rains respectively. Hence, the harvest seasons are fixed as consequence of the rainy seasons. Thus, God appointed His times among these two important cycles, in part, to demonstrate that He alone is responsible for rain and harvest; He is our Provider.

The lessons of the "appointed times" do not end there. In Israel's history, key events happened during these times of rain and harvest and, thus, God attached a significant historical event to an already existing season. This helped to ensure that His people would always remember, and hopefully keep, His feasts. The seven feasts and significant events or themes associated with them are:

- Passover: Blood of the lamb on the doorposts.
- Unleavened Bread: No time for the bread to rise.
- First fruits: Israel passing through the Red Sea.
- Pentecost: Israel receives the Torah at Mt. Sinai.
- Trumpets: Sounding trumpets / release from prison.
- Atonement: Judgement of the righteous and wicked.
- Tabernacles: Provision in the wilderness.

Among these seven feasts there are three so-called "pilgrimage feasts" during which Israel was to present themselves before the Lord. They are Unleavened Bread (Passover), Pentecost and Tabernacles. Concerning these festivals the Scripture declares:

"Three times a year all your males shall appear before the LORD your God in the place which He chooses: at the Feast of Unleavened Bread, at the Feast of the Weeks, and at the Feast of Tabernacles; and they shall not appear before the LORD empty handed."
- Deuteronomy 16:16

These three feasts commemorate three significant events in Israeli history. Unleavened Bread reminds us of the Exodus from Egypt: Pentecost signifies the giving of the Torah at Mt. Sinai; and Tabernacles is a memorial to how God preserved Israel in the wilderness. Tabernacles is also the time when Solomon dedicated the First Temple in Jerusalem. All of these events are extremely important in the history of Israel.

Still, these special times are much more than historical events. Though many Christians see them as nothing more than something Christ has fulfilled - and consequently, they assume, there is no need to bother with them - the truth of the matter is, these feasts are pictures of the earth's cycles from creation to the future Messianic kingdom. In other words, these things that happened in the past are written as an example to those of us living in the last days. Therefore, if the patterns of these feasts affect us, should we not better understand them?

Many students of Scripture are of the opinion that the first four feasts - Passover, Unleavened Bread, Firstfruits and Pentecost - were fulfilled 2,000 years ago and in chronological order. With his death, burial and resurrection, Jesus fulfilled the feasts of Passover, Unleavened Bread and Firstfruits. Fifty days after His resurrection the outpouring of the Holy Spirit, in Acts 2, fulfilled the feast of Pentecost.

Because these have been fulfilled in this manner, people presume that the final fall feasts will be fulfilled by Christ and in chronological order as well. I agree with this logic. However, I will add that **all** seven of these feasts have been fulfilled in some way, and even though they have been fulfilled, all of these feasts have a future fulfillment as well. In other words, the historical events attached to these seven festivals, including how Christ fulfilled them, hint at end time events. Solomon recorded that:

> "That which has been is what will be; that which is done is what will be done: and there is nothing new under the sun. Is there anything of which it may be said, 'See, this is new'? It has already been in ancient times before us." - Ecclesiastes 1:9-10

In short, there are prophetic mysteries hidden in the feasts of Israel. Perhaps the most dramatic example of this concept among the seven feasts is the feast of Passover.

TYPES AND SHADOWS

"On the fourteenth day of the first month at twilight is the LORD's Passover." - Leviticus 23:5

Pesach or Passover, the first of the seven *moedim* as well as the first of the three pilgrimage feasts, commemorates the Exodus from Egyptian slavery because God's people trusted in the blood of a lamb. The Passover, prepared on the fourteenth day of the Hebrew month *Aviv*, marks the deliverance from oppression and the salvation of Israel. Most importantly, the Passover speaks of the Lamb of God who takes away the sins of the world by His crucifixion and subsequent resurrection. In fact, Scripture teaches that He is the very reason for all of these feasts and appointed times.

"So let no one judge you in food or in drink, or regarding a festival or a new moon or sabbaths, which are a shadow of things to come; but the substance is of Christ." - Colossians 2:16-17

First of all, let me say that this is one of those passages that is greatly misunderstood. Most theologians argue that Paul is telling the congregation at Colosse they shouldn't let anyone judge them simply because they **don't** observe new moons and sabbaths. Because these things are referred to as "shadows" - which means to many Bible students that new moons and sabbaths have no real substance - has led people to believe that it is appropriate to downplay their importance.

However, consider for a moment that maybe the Colossians did observe these things and were being judged for it. Perhaps Paul is encouraging the Colossians not to worry about the judgment of those who don't understand the new moons, sabbaths and festivals of the LORD and it is, in fact, those doing the judging who don't keep these feasts. Here is why I say this.

Even though Paul states that these sabbaths, new moons and festivals are "a shadow of things to come," we must remember that the one throwing the shadow - the substance - is Christ. The shadow is, consequently, a precise similitude of the substance. In other words, new moons, sabbaths and festivals point us to teach us about Jesus Christ. That is why we find Him in all of these patterns. Those who would be willing to dispense with the "shadows" are, in effect, trying to do away with the substance. That is why Paul encourages the Colossians not to believe the judgments of others.

Furthermore. All things that point to Christ - including sabbaths, festivals and new moons - are prophetic in nature and, consequently, will also be encoded with other future and end-time events. Thus, the Scripture says:

"Worship God! For the testimony of Jesus is the spirit of prophecy." - Revelation 19:10

The emphasis of Passover is the Exodus story; Israel's redemption and salvation by the blood of a spotless lamb. Through the deliverer Moses, God performed great miracles so that His people might be freed from Egyptian bondage. Their sojourn from Egypt would take them to the Promised Land but not before they first traversed the wilderness to receive God's Torah (Law) at Mount Sinai. In fact, it should be pointed out here that, for centuries, rabbis have tied the liberty that came at Passover to the giving of the Torah that came at Sinai. The rabbis argue that "liberty without law results in anarchy." In other words, a free man left to his own devices will not recognize any boundaries but will do whatever seems right in his heart. We need God to tell us what is acceptable behavior and what is not. Thus the Scripture warns that:

"There is a way that seems right to a man, but its end is the way of death." - Proverbs 14:12

What makes this Exodus-Mount Sinai connection even more interesting is that, the day on which God gave Israel the Ten Commandments (Exodus 19-20) was the same day that later became the feast of Pentecost. Thus, the events of Passover are linked to the events of Pentecost; the freedom the lamb provided made it possible for Israel to receive God's Word. I will address this in a bit more detail later on.

The primary passages of Scripture dealing with the Exodus story, at least as far as Passover and Pentecost are concerned, are found in Exodus chapters 12-20. In Exodus 12 we see how the Passover was to be prepared on the fourteenth day of the Hebrew month *Aviv* (Exodus 12:6); and how it is eaten on that night (Exodus 12:8). The Scripture tells us that, on that very night, the death of Egypt's firstborn led to Israel's release from slavery; and how they eventually arrived at Mount Sinai on the first day of the third month, called *Sivan* in Hebrew (Exodus 19:1). Still, there are many other details to this story that merit our attention.

CHRIST IN THE PASSOVER

First of all, Exodus chapter 12 gives great detail about the lamb that was to be sacrificed. It was to be a male lamb of the first year without blemish. It was to be taken into the house on the tenth day of the month *Aviv.* For the next four days it was to be inspected to be sure that there were no imperfections that would disqualify it from being offered as the Passover lamb. On the fourteenth day of the month, the lamb was killed "at twilight" (Exodus 12:6).

In the Hebrew text, "at twilight" is the phrase הערבים בין *bein ha'arvayim* or literally, "between the evenings." This has been interpreted as meaning that the lamb was to

79

be sacrificed between the evening oblations or sacrifices. In the days of the Temple, and presumably before that, daylight hours were quartered; six until nine, nine until noon were the morning oblations; noon until three, three until six were the evening oblations. The nexus of the evenings or "between the evenings" would be about three o'clock in the afternoon (which would also be considered as the "ninth hour" counting from six in the morning).

On this first Passover at the appointed time, the father of the house would gather his family, take the lamb to the door of the house and slaughter it. According to tradition, the blood was drained into the basin at the door of the house. Then taking a hyssop branch as his brush, he would apply the blood to the lintel and doorpost of his home. Again according to tradition, the blood was applied in the form of the letter *tav*, which in ancient times resembled a cross. According to Scripture, it was the blood that was going to protect them from the plague coming upon Egypt's firstborn.

"Now the blood shall be a sign for you on the houses where you are. And when I see the blood, I will pass over you; and the plague shall not be on you to destroy you when I strike the land of Egypt."

- Exodus 12:13

Now it should be understood that the meaning of the LORD's Passover is not that He would "pass by" the house when He saw the blood, but that He would "pass over" the house. According to the Scripture, not only did the Lord pass through Egypt that night, but the destroyer passed through the land as well (Exodus 12:23). However, the destroyer was not permitted to enter the homes of those who had placed the blood upon their door. In fact, God saw it by "passing over" their door.

If the LORD were going to "pass over" in the sense that He was going to pass one house and go on to another, the Hebrew word that should have been used is עבר *avar*. Yet, the Hebrew word פסח *pasach* is used here and literally means to "spread wings over." We see this meaning in a passage found in the book of Isaiah.

"Like birds flying about, so will the LORD of hosts defend Jerusalem. Defending, He will also deliver it; passing over, He will preserve it." - Isaiah 31:5

The Hebrew word translated here as "passing over" is פסח *pasoach*; the root word being פסח *pasach*, from which we get פסח *pesach* or Passover (notice that all three words are spelled identically in Hebrew). The point, is when the LORD "passes over" Jerusalem, it is like a "bird flying"; the passing over infers that His wings are spread over Jerusalem in order to defend and protect it.

So in the case of the death of the firstborn, when God saw the token of the covenant, the blood, He spread His wings over that home and prevented the destroyer from entering. Therefore, the meaning of the Lord's Passover is not that he passed by the blood-sprinkled house, but that Jesus stood at the door and kept the destroyer out - all because of the blood of the lamb!

After the blood had been applied to the door, the lamb's carcass was prepared for roasting. The Scripture says that every part of the lamb had to be roasted including the head and its entrails (Exodus 12:9). Everyone knows that meat which is meant to be eaten should not be cooked with the entrails still intact. So, tradition says that the lamb was gutted and the entrails wrapped around its head. Then two sticks were used - one horizontally and one vertically - to impale the lamb making it suitable for roasting. In other words, the lamb was placed upon a cross of sorts with its entrails wrapped around its head!

Every aspect of the lamb's death and the importance of its blood points us to Christ and our salvation through Him.

The Passover lamb had to be a male lamb without spot or blemish. Concerning Christ, Scripture records that:

"The next day John saw Jesus coming toward him, and said, 'Behold! The Lamb of God who takes away the sin of the world.' " - John 1:29

"You were not redeemed with corruptible things, . . . but with the precious blood of Christ, as of a lamb without blemish and without spot." - 1 Peter 1:18-19

The lamb was taken into the house on the tenth day of Aviv to be inspected for imperfections and finally, when it was deemed a suitable sacrifice, the lamb was killed at about 3 o'clock in the afternoon of the fourteenth day of Aviv. According to the Scriptures, Jesus fulfilled each of these details.

We know that, just days before His death, Jesus rode into Jerusalem upon a donkey's colt to the cries and cheers of "Hosanna to the son of David. Blessed is he who comes in the name of the Lord" (Matthew 21:9). This event is what we refer to as the Triumphal Entry that occurred on what is now called Palm Sunday. Interestingly enough, we can prove from Scripture (most notably John 12) that this occurred on the same day that the Passover lamb was being escorted into the Temple in preparation for its sacrifice. This would have been the tenth day of Aviv.

We are also told in Scripture that from this time until the time of His execution, Jesus was being drilled with questions in an attempt to find some flaw in His answer and thus find fault with Him.

"Then the Pharisees went and plotted how they might entangle Him in His talk." - Matthew 22:15

Nevertheless we see that their plot failed and, not only that, we also learn that when He quizzed them about the Scripture they were forced to keep silent. In the end, it was not His faults that were exposed, but theirs. And so the Scripture records that:

"And no one was able to answer Him a word, nor from that day on did anyone dare question Him any-more." - Matthew 22:46

Still, they pushed for His death and eventually handed Him over to Pilate for execution. Yet, it is the exe-cutioner who is forced to say:

"I find no fault in Him at all." - John 18:38

He was found to be the spotless lamb after being inspected from the moment He entered into the house of His Father until the very moment He was led to the slaughter.

According to Exodus 12, the lamb was to be killed "between the evenings." The Scripture is very clear about what time Christ was taken to be scourged, when He was led to Golgotha and what time He finally expired.

"Now it was the third hour, and they crucified Him." - Mark 15:25

"Now it was the Preparation Day of the Passover, and about the sixth hour. And he said to the Jews, 'Behold your King!' But they cried out, 'Away with Him' . . . Then they took Jesus and led Him away."
- John 19:14-16

"Now from the sixth hour until the ninth hour there was darkness over all the land. And about the ninth hour Jesus cried out with a loud voice, saying, 'Eli, Eli, lama sabachthani?' . . . And Jesus cried out again with a loud voice, and yielded up His spirit."
- Matthew 27:45-46, 50

The Scripture paints a picture whereby we understand that Jesus was taken to Pilate early in the morning to be judged; then taken to be scourged at about nine o'clock in the morning - the third hour. At about the same time, according to tradition, the lamb that had been in the Temple compound for the previous four days was taken and tied "to the horns of the altar" to await its execution (Psalm 118:27). It was also during this time that the soldiers who whipped Jesus took thorns and fashioned a crown for His head, reminiscent of the first passover lamb.

At about noon, Jesus was led to Golgotha and hung upon the tree, suffering there for the next three hours, suffocating and slowly bleeding to death. The wounds that caused the massive loss of blood were in His feet, His hands and upon His head. The other wound in His side came after he was already dead (John 19:34). These three points on His body remind us of the blood that was at the foot of the door and the blood posted on the lintel and two doorposts of the Hebrew homes in Egypt.

When the Lord passed through the land of Egypt and saw the blood upon the house, He said He would "pass over" them and that is to say, as we have learned, that He would spread His wings over them to protect them. Just days before His death, Jesus alludes to this first Passover when He said:

"O Jerusalem, Jerusalem, the one who kills the prophets and stones those who are sent to her! How often I wanted to gather your children together, as a hen gathers her chicks under her wings, but you were not willing! See! Your house is left to you desolate."
- Matthew 23:37-38

Keep in mind, He said this just days before Passover. The fact that He wanted to extend His wings but Jerusalem was not willing, must mean that the children were not protected. Consequently, their house was left without children - desolate.

Still, the fact that He did extend His arms upon the cross to be crucified means that you and I have the gift of liberty, salvation and redemption. Just as the blood of the lamb protected Israel from the destroyer, so too does the blood of the Lamb protect us from the Adversary. Not only that; Scripture teaches us that those who partook of the Passover left Egypt completely disease free.

"If you diligently heed the voice of the LORD your God and do what is right in His sight, . . . I will put none of the diseases on you which I have brought on the Egyptians. For I am the LORD who heals you."

- Exodus 15:26

Likewise, the Scripture relates to us that the blood of Messiah, the Lamb of God, has the power to protect His people from disease and other sufferings.

"Who Himself bore our sins in His own body on the tree, that we, having died to sins, might live for righteousness - by whose stripes you were healed."

- 1 Peter 2:24

Understanding the healing benefit of the Passover now leads us to one of the greatest promises made to the end-time generation.

THE PASSOVER ORDER

When Israel sat down to eat the Passover, they also

partook of *matzah* or unleavened bread; this is what the LORD had commanded. As I mentioned earlier, Passover actually initiates the Feast of Unleavened Bread, an appointed time which lasts for seven days. This period of seven days teaches that those who have been saved by the blood of the Lamb (the Passover) should:

"Purge out the old leaven, that you may be a new lump, since you truly are unleavened. For indeed Christ, our Passover, was sacrificed for us."
- 1 Corinthians 5:7

In other words, because we have been saved by the blood of the Lamb, we are to expunge those things from our lives that are contrary to the will of God. This is to say, "Now that you have been born again, walk in obedience." When we do this, we have the promise of deliverance from the Adversary and from all the "diseases of Egypt."

I feel it is important to point out that knowing about these principles is important, but to experience them is even more important. In other words. we should:

"Be doers of the Word, and not hearers only."
- James 1:22

Likewise, Paul wrote:

"For not the hearers of the law are just in the sight of God, but the doers of the law will be justified."
- Romans 2:13

If Israel had placed the blood of the lamb upon their doors but had not eaten the lamb or the *matzah* and bitter herbs, would they have been considered obedient? Perhaps they would still have been saved from Egyptian bondage, but would they have left Egypt in a healthy state? Would they have experienced abundant living?

That being said, I believe it is important to look at the other elements of the Passover, primarily the *matzah* (unleavened bread) and bitter herbs, by briefly describing the elements of the Passover Seder.

First of all the Hebrew word סדר *seder* (pronounced *say-der*) means "order." So, a *seder* is simply the order of the service. Through the centuries, the *seder* has been written down so that all of the customs could be preserved for every generation. Consequently, the Passover service of today will closely resemble the service of centuries ago.

On today's Passover table, one will find the *matzah* (unleavened bread) and bitter herbs of course, but along with it you will find other elements intended to teach of important components in the Passover story. I have listed the most important of these elements and their relevance to the Passover story below.

Karpas: Usually a sprig of parsley intended to serve as a reminder of the hyssop branch.

Salt Water: Used to remind us of the tears shed in bondage. Also, the *karpas* is dipped into the salt water to remind us of how Israel passed through the sea and emerged free people, i.e. "born again."

Maror: "Bitter herbs" used to recall the bitterness of bondage. Oftentimes this is horseradish and/or bitter lettuce.

Charoset: A mixture of apples, nuts and cinnamon, intended to resemble the brick and mortar Israel was forced to make for Pharaoh.

Zeroah: Literally "arm" but represented by the shank bone of a lamb. Because there is no standing Temple to sacrifice in, there is no lamb on the table. The shank bone is to remind us that the death of a lamb was necessary for us to be made free.

It is customary to have, along with these items, four cups of wine. The basis for these four cups is four promises God made to Israel as He was preparing to deliver them from Egypt.

"Therefore say to the children of Israel, 'I am the LORD; I will bring you out from under the burdens of the Egyptians; I will rescue you from their bondage, and I will redeem you with an outstretched arm and with great judgments. I will take you as My people, and I will be your God . . . and I will bring you into the land which I swore to give to Abraham, Isaac and Jacob and I will give it to you as a heritage. I am the LORD.' "

- Exodus 6:6-8

Thus, the four cups of wine and what they represent are:

- Cup of Sanctification: "I will bring you out."
- Cup of Affliction: "I will rescue you from bondage"
- Cup of Redemption: "I will redeem you."
- Cup of Praise: "I will take you as My people."

The third cup, the cup of Redemption, is the one which comes after supper. Jesus identified Himself with this cup. According to the Scripture:

"He also took the cup after supper saying, 'This cup is the new covenant in My blood which is shed for you.' " - Luke 22:20

In some Passover seders, the fourth cup is also called Elijah's cup. This cup is prophetic in nature and looks to the coming of the Messiah because, as Scripture foretells, Elijah will announce Messiah's arrival. It is customary during the *seder* to set a place for Elijah and for the children to open the door to look for his arrival. This prophetic theme inherent in the Passover is seen when Christ, at the beginning of the Last Supper (which was a Passover Seder) said to His disciples:

" 'With fervent desire I have desired to eat this Passover with you before I suffer; for I say to you: I will no longer eat of it until it is fulfilled in the kingdom of God.' Then He took the cup, and gave thanks, and said, 'Take this and divide it among ourselves, for I say to you: I will not drink of the fruit of the vine until the kingdom of God comes.' " - Luke 22:15-18

Because there is no legitimate reason to believe that Jesus ate the Passover with His disciples **after** He suffered, the question is, "When will the Passover be completely fulfilled?" Furthermore, if He is going to drink of the fruit of the vine when the Kingdom comes, when exactly will that be? In other words, what prophetic event is being hinted at by the supper at large and the cup of Elijah specifically?

"Then he said to me, 'Write, Blessed are those who are called to the marriage supper of the Lamb!' And he said to me, 'These are the true sayings of God.'"
- Revelation 19:9

There is only one supper in all of Scripture which focuses upon a lamb and that is the Passover. Furthermore, considering what Jesus said to His disciples on the eve of His death, sharing the Passover with His followers is something that must be done in the Kingdom when all is fulfilled. It seems to me that the marriage supper of the Lamb is the likely time for this to happen. That means when we partake of the Passover, not only are we remembering the Lord's suffering, but we are also looking forward to being with Him in the Kingdom.

One last thing needs to be pointed out concerning the cups of Passover. In some seder traditions, the cup of Elijah is distinguished from the fourth cup, the cup of Praise. In other words, some traditions have five cups at Passover. The reason for this is due to the multiple promises that God made to His people in Exodus 6. I have already listed the traditional four, but for the sake of clarity, I will list them again.

- Cup of Sanctification: "I will bring you out."
- Cup of Affliction: "I will rescue you from bondage"
- Cup of Redemption: "I will redeem you."
- Cup of Praise: "I will take you as My people."

In reality, God actually promised five things. After He promised to take them as His people, He further promised to bring them into the land of their fathers.

"And I will bring you into the land which I swore to give to Abraham, Isaac and Jacob and I will give it to you as a heritage. I am the LORD." - Exodus 6:8

That Elijah is connected to this promise is significant because Elijah comes before the "great and dreadful day of the LORD" in order to "turn the hearts of the children to their fathers" (Malachi 4:5-6). The ultimate fulfillment of this is to bring the children back into an understanding of the fathers culminating in a return to the land of the fathers. In other words, the promise to bring Israel into the land is **not limited** to what happened under the supervision of Joshua the son of Nun, but actually speaks of what will happen at the end of the age. In short, the things that have happened will happen yet again. It is clear that the Feasts of the LORD are prophetic in nature.

THIS IS MY BODY

At this point, the unleavened bread of Passover needs to be discussed in a more exhaustive manner. As has been noted earlier, Passover initiates a week of eating unleavened bread exclusively. Today most *matzah* is made in factories on machines that produce a square-shaped piece of bread. In ancient times, the *matzah* was made at home on a grill and, according to some traditions, was triangular in shape and according to others, it was circular.

Whatever the shape may have been or has become, the one thing about the *matzah* that has remained constant is that it contains no leaven. Then as now, precautions were taken to insure that the bread would not rise. To have leaven in the house during the feast of unleavened bread was and is serious business; you could be cut off from the community of believers (Exodus 12:15). So through the years, it became customary for families seeking to be faithful to this command to commence clearing their houses of leaven weeks before the advent of Passover.

This tradition would climax on the night before the Passover. On this night the family would search the house for the last remaining crumbs of leaven using only candles for light. When the crumbs were located a member of the family would take a feather and sweep the leaven into a wooden spoon and then place it in a bag. The bag would be taken outside the house the next morning and burned, signifying that they had faithfully removed all traces of leaven from their house.

When Jesus and His disciples left the upper room, they went into the Garden of Gethsemane where Jesus prayed until His sweat became blood. While there, He determined once and for all to go to the cross, denying His own will so that the will of the Father might be accomplished. As a result of His commitment we are told that

Jesus became the "leaven" so that we could be made righteous.

"He made Him who knew no sin to be sin for us, that we might become the righteousness of God in Him." - 2 Corinthians 5:21

Soon after Jesus concluded His prayers in the garden, a band of guards carrying torches, wooden staves and clubs came into the garden searching for Him. When they found Him they took Him to the High Priest for trial. On the next morning, He was led outside of the city and executed. In other words, even in the traditional search for leaven, we see the story of the crucifixion. It also becomes apparent that the bread of Passover is representative of Christ.

As I mentioned earlier, in ancient times unleavened bread was made on a grill. After the dough was kneaded it was quickly placed on a grill to be cooked. To insure that the bread would not ferment and develop leaven, sharp pins were used to pierce the dough. The end result was bread that was unleavened, but also striped and pierced with holes. Even with today's modern methods of manufacturing *matzah*, the traditional look has been preserved. The *matzah* is made in such a way that it is still striped and punctured with holes. In short, it is a picture of the suffering Messiah.

"He was wounded for our transgressions; He was bruised for our iniquities; the chastisement for our peace was upon Him, and by His stripes we are healed."
- Isaiah 53:5

"They pierced My hands and My feet."
- Psalm 22:16

"Then they will look on Me whom they pierced. Yes, they will mourn for Him as one mourns for his only son, and grieve for Him as one grieves for a firstborn."
- Zechariah 12:10

Traditionally, three pieces of *matzah* are used during the Passover and are typically contained in a bag commonly referred to as a "unity bag" which results in three being one: a tri-unity. There are multiple reasons given for the use of three pieces of *matzah* to be used in this manner The most common explanations are that the three *matzot* represent the:

- Priests, the Levites and the rest of Israel.
- Three patriarchs: Abraham, Isaac and Jacob.
- Three angels who appeared to Abraham.
- Three chambers of the Temple.

When you consider that the middle piece of *matzah* is known as the "bread of affliction" and will be broken in two during the Passover, it becomes clear which of these traditions makes the most sense. In other words, what would be the significance of the Levites being broken? Why would it be necessary to portray the second angel or the inner court of the Temple being broken? But if the middle piece of *matzah* corresponds to the middle patriarch, Isaac, then the picture comes into focus.

As I mentioned earlier in the book, Isaac was the promised seed, born of a womb that had to be opened miraculously. He was referred to as Abraham's "only son." He carried the tree upon his back to the top of the mountain in order to be lifted up as a sacrifice. He is a picture of Christ.

When the middle piece of *matzah* is broken, one part of it is eaten while the remaining piece is wrapped in linen and hidden. Later in the *seder*, after supper, this hidden piece of *matzah* will be "resurrected" and will be referred to as the *afikomen* or "that which comes after." Furthermore, after this piece of *matzah* is removed from the linen and eaten, it is considered to be representative of the lamb. Jesus identified Himself with this piece of *matzah* when He said:

"This is My body which is given for you; do this in remembrance of Me." - Luke 22:19

THE PROMISE OF THE FATHER

The fact that the *afikomen* is first broken, then wrapped in linen, buried and ultimately resurrected is dramatic enough. Nevertheless, there is yet another prophetic component to this piece of bread.

Centuries ago, a custom developed that centered around the hidden *afikomen*. Because it did come to represent the lamb, thus becoming the most important part of the ceremony, unless the *afikomen* was found and unwrapped the *seder* could not conclude. The custom, therefore, was to have the children search for the hidden *afikomen*. When it was discovered the one who found it could bargain for something in exchange for the *afikomen*.

After the bargain was agreed upon, the father would give a token monetary gift in exchange for the all-important *afikomen*. Along with the token came the father's promise that there was more to come - the big prize that comes after. This promise came to be known as the "Promise of the Father."

And so we see that the bread which came down from Heaven, that is Christ (John 6:41), was broken for us and was wapped in linen.

"And Nicodemus, who at first came to Jesus by night, also came bringing a mixture of myrrh and aloes, about a hundred pounds. Then they took the body of Jesus, and bound it in strips of linen with the spices, as the custom of the Jews is to bury." - John 19:39-40

"So they both ran together, and the other disciple outran Peter and came to the tomb first. And he, stooping down and looking in, saw the linen cloths lying there; yet he did not go in." - John 20:4-5

When the "children" found Him, He was "unwrapped."

"Then they (the two angels) said to her, 'Woman, why are you weeping?' She said to them, 'Because they have taken away my Lord and I do not know where they have laid Him.' Now when she had said this, she turned around and saw Jesus standing there and did not know

that it was Jesus." - John 20:13-14

When it was revealed to the disciples that He indeed was alive - He appeared to them for forty days; from the Feast of Firstfruits until ten days before Pentecost - they desired that He should remain with them. However, as He had already explained to them before His death, it was necessary for Him to go (John 16:7). But before He left, He made them the promise of a special gift.

"Behold, I send the Promise of My Father upon you, but tarry in the city of Jerusalem until you are endued with power from on high." - Luke 24:49

Thus we learn that the death of the Lamb at Passover made it possible for the "promise of the Father," which is the Holy Spirit, to come. This is the gift that Christ promised to all of those who believe (Acts 2:38). Of course we see that this did, indeed, come to pass fifty days after His resurrection, when "the day of Pentecost had fully come" and the children received the gift (Acts 2:1).

Chapter Five

FROM REDEMPTION TO RESURRECTION

"Most assuredly, I say to you, unless a grain of wheat falls into the ground and dies, it remains alone, but if it dies, it produces much grain." - John 12:24

I mentioned earlier that rabbis have long connected Passover to the Feast of Pentecost. In fact, to accentuate this connection, Pentecost has been deemed an *atzeret* or solemn assembly - a day which brings a close to the season that Passover initiated. So, the giving of the Torah (the Word) at Sinai was the fruit of what was begun at Passover.

We should understand that this connection is more than something rabbis concocted - it is a connection God intended. In fact, He tells Israel to:

"Count fifty days to the day after the seventh Sabbath: then you shall offer a new grain offering to the LORD. You shall bring from your dwellings two wave

loaves of two-tenths of an ephah. They shall be of fine flour; they shall be baked with leaven. They are the firstfruits to the LORD." - Leviticus 23:16 - 17

This counting begins on the Feast of Firstfruits, a day that comes during the Feast of Unleavened Bread. It is the day when Israel would come and present unto God the firstfruits of their grain harvest, typically barley. Thus, the counting (it is called the counting of the omer) links the first harvest of grain with the second harvest of grain, i.e. Pentecost.

The Feast of Firstfruits was the same day that Christ was resurrected and became the "firstfruits of those who have fallen asleep" (1 Corinthians 15:20). The Scripture records that when He came forth from the tomb, the saints who had fallen asleep were resurrected along with Him. So, at the same time the men of Israel were preparing to present the firstfruits of their harvest unto the LORD, Christ was presenting His firstfruits unto God. This was made possible because of what He did at Passover.

According to His own words, Christ connected the death of God's Lamb to the fruit that would come at Pentecost. He was the grain of wheat that went into the ground and died so that much fruit could be realized at Pentecost, fifty days after His resurrection.

That is, in fact, what Pentecost means - "fiftieth." Fifty days after Israel crossed the Red Sea, God came down upon Mount Sinai in the sight of all the people and gave them His Torah, His Law (Exodus 19 - 20). He had already saved them by the blood of the Lamb, but before He would allow them to enter the land He had promised them, He brought them instructions on how to live.

"You have seen what I did to the Egyptians, and how I bore you on eagles' wings and brought you to Myself. Now therefore, if you will indeed obey My voice and keep My covenant, then you shall be a special treasure to Me above all people, for all the earth is Mine. And you shall be to Me a kingdom of priests and a holy nation. These are the words which you shall speak to the children of Israel." - Exodus 19:4-6

So, we learn that Passover is about redemption, salvation, and protection. Yet we also learn that Passover is about departing - departing bondage and the ways of the nations. At Sinai, a saved and liberated people had to learn to live as saved and liberated people. In short, God gave the Torah to teach God's people how God's people are to live.

FROM SINAI TO MORIAH

There is a tradition that the stone upon which the Ten Commandments were written originally came from Mount Moriah. This is interesting for several reasons; first of all, because מריה "Moriah" is related to the Hebrew word מורה *moreh* which means "teacher." The giving of the Law was to "teach" Israel how to live so that they could enter the Promised Land as a "kingdom of priests." The second reason this tradition is so interesting is because of the parallels between what happened at Sinai and what happened in Jerusalem and the outpouring of the Spirit in Acts 2.

When Jesus promised to send the Holy Spirit, He emphasized the fact that the Spirit of God would be sent as our teacher, our *Moreh*.

"For the Holy Spirit will teach you in that very hour what you ought to say." - Luke 12:12

"But the Helper, the Holy Spirit, whom the Father will send in My name, He will teach you all things, and bring to your remembrance all things that I said to you." - John 14:26

So we see that the giving of the Torah at Sinai and the outpouring of the Holy Spirit are parallel events. Here are some of the parallels I have considered. First, Moses went up to Mount Sinai while Christ's disciples waited on Zion and went to the Temple Mount. The people saw fire on the mountaintop and heard the voice of God speak.

In fact, according to tradition, when God began to speak, His voice was seen as tongues of fire dividing into every language then known to man. In Acts 2, cloven or divided tongues of fire were witnessed as the disciples began to speak in other tongues. The Bible says that they spoke in "every language under heaven" (Acts 2:5-8).

Moses received the law written upon tablets of stone where the disciples in Acts 2, and all those who have followed, received the Spirit of God who wrote the Law upon their hearts.

"Behold, the days are coming, says the LORD, when I will make a new covenant with the house of

Israel and with the house of Judah . . . This is the covenant that I will make with the house of Israel after those days, says the LORD; I will put My law in their minds, and write it on their hearts, and I will be their God, and they shall be My people." - Jeremiah 31:31,33

Notice also that, after Moses received the Tablets of the Law, Israel fashioned a golden calf according to the manner of the Egyptians. The result was that 3,000 died of the plague (Exodus 33:28). On the day of Pentecost 3,000 were saved and baptized in the name of Jesus Christ (Acts 2:41).

If they are parallel events then that means they served the same purpose because, in each case, the death of the Lamb had made it all possible. Yes, the giving of the Law and the outpouring of the Spirit are connected in that both events were intended to teach God's people how to behave.

Some might be tempted to say what happened at Sinai was just a shadow of what was to come. True, but remember who casts the shadow - Christ. Furthermore, I think everyone would agree that the Spirit of Truth will never lead God's people into something that contradicts the Word of Truth; He will teach the same things revealed in God's Word. As a matter of fact, look at what Scripture teaches the Holy Spirit will accomplish when He is within us.

"I will give you a new heart and put a new spirit within you; I will take the heart of stone of your flesh and give you a heart of flesh. I will put My Spirit with-

in you and cause you to walk in My statutes, and you will keep My judgments and do them. Then you shall dwell in the land that I gave to your fathers, you shall be My people, and I will be your God."- Ezekiel 36:26-28

The Father promised to place his Spirit within His people causing them to walk according to His statutes - His laws. When they learned to walk in obedience, "then" He said, His people would dwell in the Promised Land. This was the purpose at Sinai, but this was also the purpose in Acts 2. The Holy Spirit dwells within us to teach us of God's ways and to help us with our weaknesses (Romans 8:26) so that we might be prepared to enter the Promised Land.

In case you are thinking that this sounds like what He has promised to do for the Jews only, you need to understand that on Pentecost, two loaves of unleavened bread were brought to the Temple and waved before the LORD. The two loaves of unleavened bread - they are not without sin as was the Messiah - represent those who are Jews and those who have been born again into the household of God through the Messiah. Paul makes this clear for us.

"Therefore, remember that you, once Gentiles in the flesh . . . that at the time you were without Christ, being aliens from the commonwealth of Israel and strangers from the covenants of promise, having no hope and without God in their world. But now in Christ Jesus you who once were far off have been brought near by the blood of Christ. For He Himself is our peace, who has made both one, and has broken down the middle

wall of separation, . . . so as to create in Himself one new man from the two, thus making peace . . . Now, therefore you are no longer strangers and foreigners, but fellow citizens with the saints and members of the household of God." - Ephesians 2:11-15, 19

Thus, we learn the death of the Lamb at Passover leads to the harvest of Pentecost. At Pentecost we see that two loaves are presented to the LORD and that those two loaves are intended to be as one. That means that those who come to Messiah regardless of their ethnicity or cultural background become one with His people Israel, and are thus entitled to the same promises just as they are expected to live according to God's standards. That is the work of the Blood and the Spirit.

FROM REDEMPTION TO SANCTIFICATION

Most of us understand the concept of redemption - something of value is used to "redeem" or buy back something else considered to be of equal value. Fewer, I believe, understand that redemption and sanctification work hand-in-hand, at least from a Biblical point of view. For example, in Exodus 13 God called upon Israel to:

"Consecrate to Me all the firstborn, whatever opens the womb among the children of Israel, both of man and beast, it is Mine . . . You shall set apart to the LORD all that open the womb, that is, every firstborn that comes from an animal which you have, the males shall be the LORD's . . . . So it shall be, when your son asks you in time to come, saying, 'What is this?' that you shall say to him, 'By strength of hand the LORD brought us out of Egypt, out of the house of bondage. And it came to pass, when Pharaoh was stubborn about letting us go, that the LORD killed all the firstborn in the land of Egypt, both the firstborn of man and the firstborn of beast. Therefore I sacrifice to the LORD all males that open the womb, but all the firstborn of my sons I redeem.' " - Exodus 13:2, 12, 14-15

The Hebrew word that is translated here as "consecrate" is קדש *kadesh*. Many times this word is translated as "holy" because to be holy, from a Hebraic perspective, is to be separated out, to be set apart. The greater inference is to be separated from the ways of the nations, or in other words, to be separated from sin.

Because death claimed the firstborn of Egypt, God placed claims upon the firstborn of Israel - the animals were to be sacrificed and the sons of Israel were to be redeemed with a lamb and then "set apart" or sanctified - they were the LORD's. In fact, it was the **firstborn** - not the second or third-born of Israel - who had been saved by the blood of the lamb!

Because we have been redeemed, we are to be "set apart." To be set apart means that we are to conduct ourselves in a manner that our Heavenly Father prescribes. In short, we are to walk in obedience to His instructions. Yes, we have been saved and have been delivered from the guilt of sin, yet it is still up to us to remove the presence of sin from our lives. Christ has given us the power to quit practicing sin and "to become children of God" (John 1:12).

It should be noted that when the LORD had redeemed His people from Egyptian bondage, He brought them into the barrenness of the wilderness. It seems that He wanted to physically "set them apart" from what they had known so that He could put His Word into them. In fact, in Exodus 13, He tells Moses that the purpose of the redemption and sanctification of the firstborn is so:

"That the LORD's law may be in your mouth, for with a strong hand the LORD has brought you out of Egypt." - Exodus 13:9

Furthermore, Scripture tells us that He led them through the wilderness because if He had led them to Canaan by way of the Philistines, they would have encountered armed resistance and would have been tempted to return to Egypt. For Israel, Egypt was a place that would distance them from God's purposes by infusing them with the ways and practices of the Gentiles.

PROTECTION AFTER REDEMPTION

As desirous as God was that His people forever leave Egypt, He knew beforehand that Egypt would be hesitant to let them go. That is why God brought ten disastrous plagues upon them. Yet after the destruction they had seen, astonishingly, Egypt still wanted to bring Israel back under their control. Knowing this in advance, God used this against them to utterly destroy them in the sight of all Israel.

"For Pharaoh will say of the children of Israel, 'They are bewildered by the land, the wilderness has closed them in.' Then I will harden Pharaoh's heart, so that he will pursue them, and I will gain honor over Pharaoh and over all his army, that the Egyptians may know that I am the LORD." - Exodus 14:3-4

It is the Adversary's constant strategy to try and entangle God's people in bondage after they have been set free. This is what he attempted through Pharaoh and this is what he tries to do even in our day. In fact, the apostle Paul warned us of this.

"Stand fast therefore in the liberty by which Christ has made us free, and do not be entangled again with a yoke of bondage." - Galatians 5:1

Even though God hardened his heart, there is no mistaking that Pharaoh was a vessel of the Adversary. Considering that he took **600** chariots and chosen men and **six** is the number of man, the armies Pharaoh sent to seize Israel were no less than the minions of Satan himself. Do not forget that Satan has troops (Ephesians 6:12).

But when Pharaoh sent armies to destroy them, God set the pillar of fire between Israel and Egypt's chariots and kept Pharaoh at bay. Scripture tells us that for Israel the pillar provided light but for the Egyptians there was darkness (Exodus 14:19-20).

Without a doubt, Satan will attempt to destroy those who have been redeemed by the blood of the Lamb and will attempt to prevent then from receiving God's Word. But

Paul encouraged us to take note of the fact that:

"You brethren are not in darkness, so that the Day should overtake you as a thief. You are all sons of light and sons of the day. We are not of the night nor of darkness." - 1 Thessalonians 5:4-5

Echoing what God said to Moses of Israel in Exodus 19, Peter said:

"But you are a chosen generation, a royal priesthood, a holy nation, His own special people, that you may proclaim the praises of Him who called you out of darkness into His marvelous light." - 1 Peter 2:9

What is His marvelous light?

"Your Word is a lamp to my feet and a light to my path." - Psalm 119:105

The Word of God gives light, and that light enables God's people to proceed forward into His purposes. Furthermore, the Spirit of God gives us understanding of the Word and all of its hidden riches (1 Corinthians 2:10).

When the priests of old needed an answer from God, the Scripture says that they would inquire of the LORD by the *Urim* and *Thummim* (Ezra 2:63). The Hebrew word אורים *urim* is literally "lights"; the word תמים *thummim* is literally "perfect" but in the plural sense of the word. Therefore, some have suggested that the *urim* and *thummim* ("perfect lights") is something the priests bore on the breastplate which had to do with lights. It has been theorized that the "lights" were probably the lights of the seven-branched lamp stand, the Holy menorah. The menorah, of course, represents the illumination that comes by the Spirit of God (Revelation 4:5).

Thus we see that the Spirit and the Word go hand-in-hand. This is the message of Pentecost and this is the fruit of redemption. Those who have been redeemed are set apart to receive the Word of God and to walk in it. As they do this, they are promised protection by the Almighty. God destroyed Pharaoh because Pharaoh was attempting to destroy Israel.

Consider something else as well. God used Israel as an instrument in His hand to destroy Pharaoh. In other words, if Israel had not been the object of Pharaoh's ire, then Pharaoh would not have been destroyed. Likewise, God allows and even authorizes those who have been redeemed by the blood of the Lamb and who walk according to His Word to trample upon the serpent (Luke 10:19).

This truth becomes critically important to those who are living in the end of days.

"And they overcame him (Satan) by the blood of the lamb and by the word of their testimony."
- Revelation 12:11

Victory over the enemy comes by the blood of the Lamb and by our obedience to God's Word. Look what happened as Israel stood at the Red Sea. Moses lifted up the **rod** - the rod that would play a role in so many other wilderness miracles - just as we are to lift up the One who hung in the cross. Just before he did this, Moses declared to the people of God:

"Stand still and see the salvation *(yeshua)* **of the LORD, which He will accomplish for you today. For the Egyptians whom you see today, you shall see again no more forever. The LORD will fight for you, and you shall hold your peace." - Exodus 14:13-14**

The Hebrew word for salvation, ישוע *yeshua*, is also the Hebrew name given to Christ. And so, we are to understand that it was *Yeshua*, Jesus the Lamb of God, who fought the battle for Israel and destroyed their enemy in the sea. Likewise it is Jesus, the One who died for us who fights the battle for us when we walk in His light. You see, it was necessary that Israel first walk the path through the sea - a path that was being illuminated by the pillar of fire and cloud - before Pharaoh could be destroyed in the water!

Consider the fact that Pharaoh was destroyed by blood and by water; the blood of the lamb and the waters of the Red Sea. In contrast, Israel was saved by the same blood and by the same water. Likewise, Satan is destroyed by the very thing that saves the Body of Christ. We have been redeemed by the blood of the Lamb and sanctified by the washing of water by the Word (Ephesians 5:26). Paul wrote:

"According to His mercy He saved us, through the washing and renewing of the Holy Spirit, whom He poured out on us abundantly through Jesus Christ our Savior." - Titus 3:5-6

From the beginning until now, it is the Blood, the Word (water) and the Spirit that spell Satan's demise (1 John 5:8).

From Redemption To Resurrection

One of the primary purposes of this book is to demonstrate the prophetic nature of Scripture and specifically how events in our future can be found in ancient events. For instance, it is very possible the Passover not only teaches us of Christ's death, burial and resurrection, but might also hint at the coming Marriage Supper of the Lamb.

Likewise, the story of Pentecost - the feast that teaches of the outpouring of the Holy Spirit and giving of the Word - may also be encoded with patterns for the Resurrection.

The text tells us that when Israel arrived at Mount Sinai, God tells Moses to tell the people to:

- Sanctify themselves (Exodus 19:10)
- Be prepared on the third day (Exodus 19:11)

The reason that they needed to prepare themselves in this way is because the LORD was going to come down on the mountain in the sight of all the people.

"Then it came to pass on the third day, in the morning, that there were thunderings and lightnings, and a thick cloud on the mountain, and the sound of the

trumpet was very loud, so that all the people who were in the camp trembled . . . Now Mount Sinai was completely in smoke, because the LORD descended upon it in fire. Its smoke ascended like the smoke of a furnace and the whole mountain quaked greatly."

- Exodus 19:16, 18

Notice that the dense smoke on the mountain was present because the LORD had descended from heaven. Along with it were thunderings and lightnings. Actually the Hebrew word קלת *kolot* - translated as "thunderings" - is literally "voices." Many times in Scripture, heavenly voices sound as thunder to people on earth. Another interesting point is that there was the sound of a trumpet growing very loud. The Hebrew word used here for "trumpet" is the word שופר *shofar*, the ram's horn. As this trumpet continues to sound, notice what happens.

"And when the blast of the trumpet sounded long and became louder and louder, Moses spoke, and God answered him by voice. Then the LORD came down upon Mount Sinai, on the top of the mountain. And the LORD called Moses to the top of the mountain, and Moses went up." - Exodus 19:19-20

As the shofar gets louder, Moses calls out to God. Now the question should be asked, "Who is sounding the shofar?" It isn't Moses and it isn't the Israelites at the foot of the mountain. It seems that trumpet is being sounded by the LORD Himself. Actually, Scripture confirms that God will (and presumably has) blown the shofar.

"Then the LORD will be seen over them. And His arrow will go forth like lightening. The Lord God will blow the trumpet, and go with the whirlwinds from the south . . . The LORD their God will save them in that day." - Zechariah 9:14, 16

Notice also that the cloud of smoke on the mountain and the blowing of the shofar seems to precede the LORD's descending upon the mount, for it is after the shofar sounds and Moses calls out to God that the LORD answers him and then arrives upon the mountain. In other words, the cloud of smoke is seen and the sound of the shofar is heard as the LORD is descending. When all of this climaxes, Moses is called up. In my opinion, this is a wonderful picture of what Paul describes as being the resurrection of the Body of Christ.

"For the Lord Himself will descend from heaven with a shout, with the voice of an archangel, and with the trumpet of God. And the dead in Christ shall rise first. Then we who are alive and remain shall be caught up together with them in the clouds to meet the Lord in the air. And thus we shall always be with the Lord. Therefore comfort one another with these words."
- 1 Thessalonians 4:16-18

Interestingly enough, there are certain Jewish traditions about the feast of Pentecost that might also hint at this future event. One of these traditions has it that Enoch was translated on the day of Pentecost. One of the customary practices of Pentecost is to stay up all night studying the

Scriptures because, it is believed, at midnight the door of heaven will be opened briefly!

One of the primary Scriptures being studied during Pentecost is the book of Ruth. In fact, on the day of Pentecost the entire story of Ruth and her relationship with the kinsman redeemer, Boaz, is read in the synagogue. I find this fascinating because of its obvious message concerning Christ. Consider these parallel points.

■ Boaz was from Bethlehem.
■ Jesus was from Bethlehem.

■ Boaz was master of the harvest.
■ Jesus is the Lord of the harvest.

■ Boaz was a kinsman-redeemer.
■ Christ is the kinsman-redeemer.

Another very important feature of the story concerns what happened to the Jewess Naomi. She had lost her inheritance due to the famine and was actually living among the Gentiles in Moab. When she determines to return to her homeland her Gentile daughter-in-law joins her in spite of Naomi's admonition to turn back.

"But Ruth said, 'Entreat me not to leave you, or to turn back from following after you; For wherever you go, I will go. And wherever you lodge I will lodge. Your people shall be my people, and your God, my God' "
- Ruth 1:16

Later, Ruth the gentile will meet the Jewish kinsman-redeemer Boaz during the barley harvest (Ruth 1:22) which, of course, is the time of Passover. She will eventually marry Boaz but only after she and her mother-in-law have been redeemed by the redeemer Boaz in the presence of ten elders (Ruth 4:2). Traditionally, Boaz and Ruth were married during the time of the wheat harvest, which is Pentecost. Furthermore, their union ushered in the "throne of David." - the kingdom that would never end.

Just as Boaz restored Naomi's inheritance by taking the gentile Ruth for his bride, so will Christ restore all of Israel to her inheritance through His union with those who have grafted into the good olive tree (Romans 11:17). Like Boaz and Ruth, who are introduced to our Redeemer at Passover and, if the traditions are true, are wedded to Him at Pentecost. Let me make this point; the picture that is presented to us in the Spring feasts of Passover and Pentecost is, that after the Redemption of Passover, the Lord will come down and be joined with His bride! Exodus 19 is an amazing code which reveals that Christ will descend from Heaven with the sound of a trumpet.

There is one last point that I would like to make before moving on. In these last days, it is critical that you and I understand God's Word as never before. In the days ahead, not only will we need the redemptive power of Christ's blood working in our lives, but we will also need to be impregnated with the seed of the Word, which was given at Pentecost. This is a must if we are to fulfill God's purposes in the end times.

Chapter Six

THE MYSTERY OF THE FALL FEASTS

As we have seen, the Spring feasts are inherently prophetic. So too are the three feasts that come in the fall. All three of the remaining feasts occur in the same Hebrew month called *Tishri*. The meaning of this month is related to the idea of "looking (forward)." That is exactly what we intend to do: by examining these appointed times, it will lead us to "look forward" to the future and what it portends for those who have been redeemed by the blood of the Lamb.

The first of these three final feasts is commonly referred to as *Rosh Hashana*; the biblical name, however, is *Yom Teruah* or the Feasts of Trumpets (Numbers 29;1-6). This day is also referred to as the "Day of Judgement" as well as the "Day of Remembrance." As we will soon see, this day is a picture of the Resurrection of the saints.

The second fall feast is *Yom Kippur* or the Day of Atonement (Leviticus 16). Atonement focuses on judgment of the righteous and the wicked. According to tradition, on this day there are three books in heaven that are used in the Heavenly Court; the book of the Righteous sealed with the seal of God (Revelation 7:3); the book of the Unrighteous (Revelation 17:8) and the Book of the Intermediate - those who are not completely wicked or righteous. In my opinion, *Yom Kippur* tells of the coming Great Tribulation.

The last of the feasts is called *Sukkot* or the Feast of Tabernacles (Leviticus 23:33-34). Like the spring feasts, these fall feasts are linked to significant historical events in Israel's history. For instance, Tabernacles is a reminder of how Israel lived in the wilderness for forty years dwelling in "booths" or *sukkot*. More importantly, it is a reminder of how God provided for them during those forty years. This feast is kept for seven days.

And like the spring feasts, the fall feasts speak prophetically. Tabernacles is regarded as the Season of Joy because it celebrates the Kingdom of God on earth and the reign of Messiah for a thousand years (Revelation 20:4). Again, all of them are linked to significant events both past and present. In this chapter, we are going to focus on their future significance.

TRUMPETS AND THE RESURRECTION

There are several themes associated with the Feast of Trumpets. For our study, I will mention three, but concentrate on one primary theme.

- The resurrection of the righteous.
- The coronation of the King.

■ The marriage of the Messiah.

These are the themes we can find in the book of Revelation.

■ The resurrection of the righteous (Rev. 20).
■ The coronation of the King (Rev. 19).
■ The marriage of the Messiah (Rev. 19).

Where the resurrection is concerned, it seems that it may be hinted at very early in the book of Revelation.

"After these things I looked, and behold, a door standing open in heaven. And the first voice which I heard was like a trumpet speaking with me, saying, 'Come up here, and I will show you things which must take place after this.' Immediately I was in the Spirit, and behold, a throne set in heaven, and One sat on the throne." - Revelation 4:1-2

In this passage, a "door" understood to be a literal opening appears in heaven. This is followed by a shout to "Come up here!" This presents a picture of the Temple in Heaven being opened and the saints pouring onto the Temple platform - the Throne Room - to begin the "morning services." Is it possible that this shout is synonymous with the shout and voice of the archangel referred to by Paul in 1 Thessalonians 4:16-17? John hearing the "voice like a trumpet" reminds us that when the LORD descends from heaven, it will be with the "trumpet of God."

Since the trumpet is such an integral part of this feast, we need to mention that more than one type of trumpet is referred to in Scripture. Actually, there are three different types of trumpets; the shofar, silver trumpets and even gold trumpets.

Silver trumpets were sounded to call the camp of Israel to attention while a second blast was the order to make the journey (Numbers 10). The silver trumpets were also sounded on the year of Jubilee (Leviticus 25). On every seventh year, if the king was present, a gold trumpet was sounded.

The shofar or ram's horn was blown on feast days and on new moon to herald the beginning of the month. It was also blown to muster troops to battle and so forth. But, according to tradition, the shofar will be sounded to awaken the dead from their slumber. Thus, because a trumpet is associated with this event, it is my opinion, as well as the opinion of many other students of the Bible, that the Resurrection of the dead in Christ will occur during the Feast of Trumpets.

Concerning the resurrection and its relationship to the Feast of Trumpets, not only do we see this in the New Testament but in ancient Jewish literature as well. In the Talmud it is recorded that:

"In the month of Tishri the world was created ... and in Tishri they (the righteous) will be redeemed in the time to come." - Rosh Hashana 10b-11a

THE CONCEALMENT OF THE SAINTS

There are some ancient Jewish traditions concerning the "gate of heaven" which at times is opened for the *neu'in* or "the home taking." This idea is linked to customs associated with a Jewish wedding. The newlyweds would go into the wedding chamber and shut the door. The inference is that, before they go into the chamber, the door had been opened. Yet, when they go in, the door is shut and remains shut for the next seven days. It is said that the couple is concealed. Interestingly, the Feast of Trumpets hints at this theme of "concealment."

Isaiah saw the time of concealment and associated it with the resurrection.

"Your dead shall live; Together with my dead body they shall arise. Awake and sing, you who dwell in dust. For your dew is like the dew of herbs, and the earth shall cast out the dead. Come, my people, enter your chamber, and shut your doors behind you: Hide yourselves, as it were, for a little moment, until the indignation is past. For behold, the LORD comes out of His place to punish the inhabitants of the earth for their iniquity. The earth will also disclose her blood, and will no more cover her slain." - Isaiah 26:19-21

It seems to me that the concealment alludes to the believers being concealed during the time of tribulation, which is definitely a time of "indignation." By indignation, the text conveys the idea of "anger and rage." This certainly sounds similar to the "wrath of God" that will be poured out during the tribulation.

"If anyone worships the beast and his image, and receives his mark on his forehead or on his hand, he himself shall also drink of the wine of the wrath of God, which is poured out full strength into the cup of His indignation." - Revelation 14:9-10

Yet as Isaiah and other prophets record, God's people will enter the "chamber" and be hidden during this time of tribulation.

"Gather yourselves together, yes gather together, O undesirable nation, before the decree is issued or the day passes like chaff; Before the LORD's fierce anger comes upon you, before the day of the LORD's anger comes upon you! Seek the LORD all you meek of the earth, who have upheld His justice. Seek righteousness, seek humility. It may be that you will be hidden in the day of the LORD's anger." - Zephaniah 2:1-3

A few of the words that are used here merit special attention. First, the word translated as "gather" is a word that is used figuratively to "assemble" but is related to the idea of gathering wood or foraging for food. It seems that those who are being told to "gather" are also being admonished to prepare. This occurs before the "fierce anger of the LORD." The reason for their preparation is that they might be "hidden" in the day of God's anger. The Hebrew word translated as "hidden" is סתר *satar* and means "to be concealed" or "to be secret." It can also mean "to be absent."

It seems clear to me that God's intention for His people is that they be hidden in the day of His wrath for, as the Scripture encourages us:

"For God did not appoint us to wrath, but to obtain salvation through our Lord Jesus Christ."
- 1 Thessalonians 5:9

Another indication of this principle of being "concealed" has to do with the ten Days of Awe. Beginning on the Feast of Trumpets and concluding on the Day of Atonement is a ten day period known in Hebrew as *yamim nora im*, or the Days of Awe. It is believed that during this ten day period, the "gates of heaven" are opened to hear the repentant prayers of Israel.

In the days of the Temple, after the conclusion of the feast of Trumpets and the fast of Gedaliah (which occurs on 3 Tishri), the High Priest would enter a secluded chamber and be concealed there for the next seven days; this was during the Days of Awe. While there he rehearsed the laws and the procedures for the Day of Atonement - the day when God would judge the wicked and the righteous! The day he emerged from this concealment was the Day of Atonement.

THE DAY OF ATONEMENT

On the tenth day of the month of Tishri the Day of Atonement is observed. This is considered to be the holiest day in all of Judaism, for it is on this day that Israel would be forgiven their sins or would face judgment.

Consequently, the people fasted and stood all day in the Temple courts seeking the face of God.

I mentioned earlier that, in this day, the belief was that three sperate groups were being judged.

- The totally righteous.
- The totally unrighteous.
- The intermediate.

While making sure that he and those he represented would be written in the Book of the Righteous, the High Priest of Israel performed four primary procedures in the Temple on Yom Kippur.

The first task was to take fire from the altar of incense. The second task was to offer sacrifices and place the blood of the sacrifices in a bowl. The third procedure was to sprinkle the blood in the Holy Place and upon the mercy seat of the Ark seven times. The fourth and all-important procedure was to pronounce, "It is done." In Revelation 8:1-6, we can see the parallel of these four events proceeding in the Heavenly Temple.

The first procedure was the burning of incense, which Scripture tells us is representative of the prayers of the saints (Psalm 141:2). In Revelation 8, we are told that there are thirty minutes of silence in heaven followed by an angel (Christ) who brings a golden censor of incense along with the prayers of the saints to the golden altar. It should be noted that, in the earthly Temple, when the Priest ministered on the Day of Atonement, Jewish history records that there was a span of silence lasting about thirty minutes.

The blood that was offered by Israel's High Priest as atonement was critically important to Israel's welfare. In fact, legend has it that God provided a sign - the miracle of the scarlet thread - to show whether or not their sins had been forgiven. According to the *Sefer Aggadah* (Book of Legends), this miracle ceased to occur "a generation before the destruction of the Second House." That, of course, would have been about the time that Christ died and rose from the dead and entered into the Heavenly Temple to make eternal atonement for sin.

The writer of Hebrew records that the atoning blood of Christ is presently in Heaven.

"Not with the blood of goats and calves, but with His own blood He entered the most Holy Place once for all, having obtained eternal redemption . . . For Christ has not entered the holy places made with hands, which are copies of the true, but into heaven itself, now to appear in the presence of God for us."

- Hebrews 9:12, 24

In the book of Revelation, John reveals to us that, in the Heavenly Temple, the Ark of the Covenant is present (Revelation 11:19). The purpose in bringing this out is to accentuate the parallel between what happened in the earthly Temple and what happened in the Heavenly Temple. Because it was considered Judgement Day, no man save the High Priest was able to enter the Temple while the blood was being applied to the Ark of the Covenant. When the High Priest of Heaven, with His own blood, ministered in the Most Holy of Holies, it was before all of those who had been resurrected with Him were taken into Heaven.

Finally after all sacrifices had been made and atonement had been accomplished, the announcement came from the Priest that all was completed. This same decree comes at the end of the age and is made by a voice out of the Temple.

"Then the seventh angel poured out his bowl into the air, and a loud voice came out of the temple of heaven, from the throne, saying 'It is done!' "

- Revelation 16:17

One other interesting point concerning this final announcement: on Passover the priest would say, "It is finished" once the final lamb was offered. On the Day of Atonement he would announce, "It is done." I believe that this is demonstrating a connection between the Redemption of Passover and the Atonement of Yom Kippur. In other words, those who have been redeemed are under the atonement and protective blood of the Lamb while all those who have rejected Him are subjected to the judgment of God.

THE SEVEN THUNDERS

"Now when the seven thunders uttered their voices, I was about to write, but I heard a voice from heaven saying to me, 'Seal up the things which the seven thunders uttered, and do not write them.' "

- Revelation 10:4

In many passages of Scripture, God's voice is compared to thunder. When He spoke on Mount Sinai, His voice was as the voice of thunder (Exodus 20:18). When He spoke as Christ entered Jerusalem, to many it sounded as thunder (John 12:19). Job said that God spoke through thunder (Job 40:9).

In the passage above, John heard God speak and it was as if seven thunders uttered. Furthermore, John was told not to write what the seven thunders said. Some scholars have suggested that the seven thunders are similar to a Coptic text in which seven Greek vowels often function as a mysterious divine name. According to the *World Bible Commentary*, it sometimes appears in the form of the Greek letters "alpha" and "omega" so as to abbreviate all seven vowels. In the Coptic text this cryptic name is referred to as the "Seven Voices."

The point here is this: are the seven thunders uttering a secret name? Remember that the sacred name of God יהוה YHVH was a name that only the High Priest could utter and only on Yom Kippur. Furthermore, the Greek *Alpha* and *Omega* is equivalent to the Hebrew *Alef* and *Tav*, which is a title given only to Jesus. It seems possible, at least, that the seven thunders utter a mysterious name that is to be known by no one.

"His eyes were like a flame of fire, and on His head were many crowns: He had a name written that no one knew except Himself." - Revelation 19:12

All in all, I believe it is to be obvious that hidden within the ritual and traditions of Yom Kippur, there lies a picture of the coming judgment upon the nations, and even upon Satan Himself. This time is none other than the Great Tribulation. Immediately following Yom Kippur is the Feast of Tabernacles - the Kingdom Feast. Immediately after the Tribulation of those days, Scripture tells us that Christ will return to the earth to rule and to reign with you and with me.

GATHERING OF THE NATIONS

In the days of the Temple, the Feast of Tabernacles was considered to be not only the Kingdom Feast, but also the Feast of the Ingathering. This was symbolized by the ingathering of the fruits of trees and the field which were brought up to Jerusalem. It is understood that these fruits were to symbolize the seven types of food in Israel. This was also to signify that, in the end, God would have worshipers coming up to Jerusalem to extol Him from every nation and every continent on earth. Tabernacles was the feast that acknowledged the ingathering of all God's people.

"Then the sign of the Son of Man will appear in heaven, and then all the tribes of the earth will mourn, and they will see the son of Man coming on the clouds of heaven with power and great glory. And He will send His angels with a great sound of a trumpet and they will gather together His elect from the four winds, from one end of heaven to the other." - Matthew 24:30-31

"Also, that he would gather together in one the children of God who were scattered abroad."- Jn. 11:52

Those "scattered abroad" is intended to mean all of those living among the Gentiles. Scripture tells us that during the Millennial reign of Messiah, all nations shall go up to Jerusalem to worship the King at the Feast of Tabernacles (Zechariah 14:16). It is at this time that all who have been redeemed by the blood of the Lamb will serve Him as His Priests in a Kingdom that shall never end. This is what we are quickly moving toward. We have seen the redemption of the Passover; we have been to Pentecost. We are now in that dry period that occurs between Pentecost and the fall feasts, but we are nonetheless moving toward the sound of trumpets!

Chapter Seven

THE TRIBULATION CODES

As we have seen, the biblical feasts are infused with information that speaks primarily of Christ, and secondly of future events. Frankly, I have only dealt with the primary feast days that most Christians are somewhat familiar with. There are, in fact, other important festivals and sabbaths that teach of Christ and prophetic scenarios, i.e. the new moons and Sabbath cycles (Ezekiel 46:1). However, I will not elaborate on these here.

At this point, I do want to examine some of the lesser feasts and by that I mean, those feasts that are observed by Israel but weren't necessarily ordained by God. That is not to say, however, that God did not orchestrate the events that led to these festivals. Because of this reality, these lesser feasts should not be discounted as mere historical events just because Christianity does not perceive any real association with them. As we will see, this perception is misplaced. These festivals, like the Seven Feasts of Israel, also speak to us of Christ and of future events. The first such festival I want to address is the one called *Purim*.

"But when Esther came before the king, he commanded by letter that this wicked plot which Haman had devised against the Jews, should return on his own head, and that he and his sons should be hanged on the gallows. So they call these days Purim after the name Pur. Therefore, because of all the words of this letter, what they had seen concerning this matter, and what had happened to them, the Jews established and imposed it upon themselves and their descendants and all who join them, that without fail they should celebrate these two days every year, according to the written instructions and according to the prescribed time, that these days should be remembered and kept throughout every generation . . . that these days of Purim should not fail to be observed among the Jews and that the memory of them should not perish among their descendants." - Esther 9:25-28

After the Persians toppled the Babylonian empire, many of the Jews who had been taken captive were assimilated into Persian civilization, some of them migrating to Persia itself. (Persia is now known as Iran.) The story of Esther is believed to have occurred about thirty years before the decree that permitted the Jews to return to Israel.

The story begins with the king of Persia, being influenced by wine, calling upon his wife Vashti to perform something that she flatly refused to do. Consequently, an enraged King Ahasuerus consults his wise men who counsel him to have the queen deposed and replaced by "another who is better than she" (Esther 1:19). That woman was a young Jewish orphan known as Hadassah. Her appointment as queen merits this observation: even though God is never mentioned in the book of Esther, do we really believe that He had nothing to do with her becoming Queen Esther? Of course not. God has always orchestrated events to fulfill his purposes in history.

The rest of the story tells us **why** God made sure Hadassah (Esther) was chosen. He knew in advance that a certain Agagite by the name of Haman would be incited to kill the Jews in Persia. The reason he devised a plan to destroy them was due to his jealousy of Esther's cousin and guardian, Mordechai.

"When Haman saw that Mordechai did not bow or pay him homage, Haman was filled with wrath. But he disdained to lay hands on Mordachai alone, for they had told him of the people of Mordechai; Instead Haman sought to destroy all the Jews who were throughout the whole kingdom of Ahasuerus - the people of Mordechai." - Esther 3:6

His plan called for all Jews throughout the one hundred and twenty provinces of Persia to be gathered and killed, all in one day! The day determined, the 13th day of the twelfth month known as *Adar* (corresponding to our mid to late February through mid to late March depending on the year), had been chosen by the casting of lots or *purim* (Esther 3:7, 13). Jewish literature records that Haman was excited about this date because, traditionally,

13 Adar was the day Moses had died. Apparently, if the tradition can be trusted, Haman interpreted this as a good omen for him and a bad one for the Jews.

When it came to his hated nemesis Mordechai, Haman had special plans. Following the direction of his wife, he had gallows erected in order to hang the man he despised. The story, records, however, that his plan backfired and, in the end, Haman was hung on those very gallows and followed in death by his ten sons, also hung on the gallows.

So, how did it happen that those who sought to destroy God's people were themselves destroyed, and on the very day that they had determined to destroy the Jews? Perhaps more importantly, what message does this story convey to those of us living in the last days? The answer is found in the central character of the story - Esther.

THE HIDDEN PROPHECY

Esther is a picture of hidden things; her very name hints at this. First of all, remember that Esther was not her real name; Hadassah was her true identity. Nevertheless she became Esther, which is a name of Gentile origin, not Hebrew. In fact, אסתר Esther is the Persian equivalent to Astarte, Ashtaroth (1 Samuel 12:10) and Ishtar, who was also known at times as Easter. Depending on which culture you found her determined what she was called, but all of these names speak of the goddess of fertility. This is what Esther's name is associated with.

Still, if we read אסתר Esther as a Hebrew word instead of a transliterated name, the results are interesting.

In Hebrew the same letters translated as Esther could also be read as אסתר *esater* which means, "I will conceal." It is obvious that the one who was concealed was Hadassah; but who was the one concealing her? That answer seems obvious as well.

As I said, God is never mentioned in this book, but who can deny His workmanship in the outcome? Who determined that Hadassah should be chosen as queen? Who made sure that Mordechai found out about Haman's wicked plot? Who was it that awakened the king out of his sleep causing him to read the history of his kingdom which led to Mordechai being honored? God is the one who concealed her so that she would be positioned to be His instrument of deliverance, just as he had already done with Moses (raised as an Egyptian in the house of Pharaoh) and Joseph (viceroy to Pharaoh).

So then, Esther is the one who looked like and was believed to be a gentile to the degree that she carried the name of one of the Persian goddesses. Yet, she knew and more importantly God knew that she was one of the chosen. Not only had God chosen her, but she had been chosen queen because the previous queen had been disobedient; Vashti refused the king's invitation to come and sit at his banquet table. It is important to note that the one he chose was a virgin who was foreign to his people and that she was acknowledged as queen - she became his bride - in the seventh year of the king's reign (Esther 2:16).

When the hidden plot to destroy God's people was uncovered, it was the virgin bride who was used to deliver all of God's people. Still, it was the king who pronounced sentence upon the adversary Haman and all of his minions.

This is what I see being presented to us through this story. Scripture relates that when Christ came to His own people, they did not receive Him (John 1:11). Jesus had foretold of this and what the result of their refusal to receive Him would be.

"O Jerusalem, Jerusalem, the one who kills the prophets and stones those who are sent to her! How often I wanted to gather your children together, as a hen gathers her chicks under her wings, but you were not willing! See! Your house is left to you desolate."
- Matthew 23:37-38

This desolation occurred because they had refused to come to his banquet table.

"Then he said to his servants, 'The wedding is ready but those who were invited were not worthy. Therefore go into the highways, and as many as you find, invite to the wedding.' " - Matthew 22:8-9

Who were these that would be invited in the stead of those who had refused to come? After witnessing a Roman centurion's faith, Jesus told the Jews following Him that:

"I say to you that many will come from east and west and sit down with Abraham, Isaac and Jacob in the kingdom of heaven. But the sons of the kingdom will be cast out into outer darkness. There will be weeping and gnashing of teeth." - Matthew 8:11-12

When some of the "sons of the kingdom" refused to come sit at His banquet table, the Father invited those from the east and west to come sit at the table. He chose people who were from the "outside" to be among those who would be His bride. Outwardly, they are considered to be gentile but, like Esther, they have a secret - they have been chosen by the King.

"You did not choose Me, but I chose you and appointed you that you should go and bear fruit, and that your fruit should remain, that whatever you ask the Father in my name He may give you." - John 15:16

Those He has chosen are intended to be His bride and His bride, like Esther, must be a chaste virgin (2 Corinthians 11:2). Esther, you will recall, was married to the king of Persia in the seventh year of his reign (Esther 2:16). Prophetically speaking, the Messiah will be crowned as King on some future Rosh Hashanah - the Feast of Trumpets. Seven years later, the marriage between the bride and bridegroom will be consummated at the Marriage Supper of the Lamb.

Through Esther, God delivered His people from those who would have destroyed them. Each time they have been threatened, whether before or after the time of Esther, He has saved them from annihilation. Scripture tells us that before Christ returns, the Antichrist will seek to destroy Israel once and for all, I believe that through His bride, God will again deliver His people from those who seek to destroy them from the face of the earth (Revelation 19:14).

Haman The Antichrist

If there is to be deliverance there must be an antagonist to be delivered from. The story of *Purim* gives us a prophetic picture of who that is - the coming Antichrist and his demonic kingdom.

First of all, it should be noted that Haman is not a Persian but is called "the Agagite" (Esther 3:1). This is to say that Haman was descended from the kings of the Amalekites (1 Samuel 15:8). It is believed by most scholars that Agag was not a name but a title for the Amalekite kings just as Pharaoh was to the Egyptians. Some believe that Agag should be considered to be equivalent to Gog of Magog (Ezekiel 38:2). The reason for this is based on the fact that in Numbers 24:7, the Hebrew phrase translated "than Agag" is מאגג *m'agag*. In fact, the *Septuagint* version, a Greek translation of the Hebrew Scriptures, translates the phrase as "than Gog." The point is that Agag and the kings of the Amalekites are viewed as antagonists where Israel is concerned.

Furthermore, it is important to understand that the father of the Amalekites was a descendant of Jacob's chief foe, Esau.

"Now Timna was the concubine of Eliphaz, Esau's son, and she bore Amalek to Eliphaz. These were the sons of Adah, Esau's wife." - Genesis 36:12

This is to say that Haman was a descendant of those who hated Israel and who had consistently displayed the will to destroy the sons of Jacob. Furthermore, Scripture makes it clear that, in the end of days, the same enemies under the control of the Beast will be seeking to destroy Israel, In short, I believe that Haman is a picture of the Antichrist.

The Bible records that Haman was exalted in the kingdom to the point that he wanted people to bow down to him. The Benjamite Mordechai refused to do so and, thus, Haman set his heart against him (Esther 3:1-6). Likewise, the Antichrist will exalt himself and, through the False Prophet, will command that all people bow and worship his image (Revelation 13:15).

Consider also that the beast has **seven heads and ten horns** (Revelation 13:1) which are ten kings (Revelation 17:12; Daniel 7:24). There are **seven princes** in the king's court (Esther 1:14) before Haman is exalted over them (Esther 3:1). The story also mentions that Haman has **ten sons** (Esther 9:10-14).

According to Scripture, the Antichrist will arise from the same region that the Persians once controlled (present-day Iran, Iraq and Syria) and will seek to subjugate or kill the people of Israel. Like Mordechai, many of them will refuse to bow to their oppressor. In the end, what the Antichrist determines to do to them will come back upon his own head for Jesus will destroy him and all of the enemies of Israel when He returns.

"And then the lawless one will be revealed, whom the Lord will consume with the breath of His mouth and destroy with the brightness of His coming."
- 2 Thessalonians 2:8

Because of His devotion to His bride, the King stood up and had Haman and his ten sons killed. In the future, the King of kings will stand up and destroy the lawless one in defense of His people.

THE HIDDEN CODES

"And in Shushan the citadel the Jews killed and destroyed five hundred men. Also Parshandatha, Dalphon, Aspatha, Poratha, Adalia, Aridatha, Parmashta, Arisai, Aridai and Vajezatha - the ten sons of Haman the son of Hammedatha, the enemy of the Jews - they killed, but they did not lay a hand on the plunder. . . . Then Esther said, 'If it pleases the king, let it be granted to the Jews who are in Shushan to do again tomorrow according to today's decree, and let Haman's ten sons be hanged on the gallows.' " - Esther 9:6-10, 13

When you read this in English, it looks like nothing more than a roster of the ten sons of Haman that were executed on the gallows. However, if you were to see this passage in Hebrew, you would notice that the first, the seventh and tenth names contain a Hebrew letter that is significantly smaller than the other Hebrew letters. Those smaller Hebrew letters are ת *tav*, ש *shin* and ז *zayin*. Many people have wondered what these three smaller letters were supposed to signify.

Then on October 16, 1946, something very significant happened. On that day, eleven prominent Nazis, including Hermann Goering, were to be hung for their part in Nazi atrocities against humanity, specifically their crimes against Jews. However, just two hours before his execution was to take place, Goering committed suicide by taking a capsule of poison he had kept hidden. This last minute suicide meant that only ten of the condemned men went to the gallows.

The fascinating point of all this is that October 16, 1946 on the Hebrew calendar was 21 Tishri 5707. The Hebrew year 5707 would be written תשז (*tav, shin, zayin*) - the three small letters contained in the names of the ten sons of Haman who were hung on the gallows. Without a doubt, the story of Esther is to relate how those who seek to destroy God's people will themselves be destroyed.

During the first Gulf War in 1991, Saddam Hussein unleashed no less than thirty-nine Scud missiles on the state of Israel. His goal was to draw Israel into the war so that other Muslim nations would join the fight. Things didn't work out that way, however, and in fact, he was forced to sue for a cease fire. The war that was supposed to be the "mother of all battles" only lasted about forty days. It ended, as a matter of fact, on Purim.

Years later, President George W. Bush picked up where his father, President George H. W. Bush, had left off. Citing the need to remove any WMDs that Hussein may have had in his arsenal, Bush committed US troops to once again fight against the Butcher of Baghdad. The first engagements of Operation Iraqi Freedom began on March 18, 2003. That day was the beginning of Purim. It was, if you will, a continuation of what had started twelve years before. Furthermore, it seems that, besides removing Saddam from the picture, it has set the stage for Persia (present day Iran) to rise again.

The Rising Prince Of Persia

History teaches us that the Persian empire defeated and then swallowed up the previous world power, Babylon. Most of you are probably aware that Persia and Babylon are present day Iran and Iraq respectively. It is interesting to note that, since Saddam is gone, Iran is trying to determine the future of Iraq. Iran, a predominately Shi'ite nation, is trying to influence the majority Shi'ite population in Iraq to see to it that Western efforts to democratize Mesopotamia fail.

Not only that, but the President of Iran has threatened to wipe Israel off the map and destroy all the Jews. Let me point something out here that might surprise many of you. Obviously the Iranians of today and the Nazis of the 1930s and 1940s share the same opinion of Jews - they should be destroyed. But did you know that the present day Iranians and the Nazis of World War II era share the ideology of being part of the "master race"?

The Nazis put forth the idea that only those of pure Aryan blood were worthy to live within the borders of Germany; all others were inferior humans. Lowest on the pecking order, according to them, were the Jews. The radicals in Iran feel the same way. Here is why: until 1935, the nation we refer to as Iran was called by its ancient name Persia.

The reason it was changed to Iran was to pay homage to all of the **Aryan** tribes who had settled the region long ago. In other words, "Iran" is derived from the word "aryan." No wonder they hate Israel. This whole region hates Israel and, to a large degree, always has. No wonder the Antichrist comes out of this region of the world (Daniel 8:9).

It has been well documented that the Iranian leaders are looking for *al Mahdi* - the Islamic messiah. Those who anticipate his coming believe he will conquer the world in the name of Islam and rid the earth of infidels - namely Jews and Christians. This "coming one" fits the biblical description of the Antichrist. With that in mind, I need to point out that Scripture does not teach that this man will come as a false messiah to the Jews as many have stated. To the contrary, the Bible teaches that this man, true to the nature of his predecessors, will try to kill all of Israel. If he does come from this region, and I am convinced that he does, he will most likely be Muslim. [For more information, see my book, *Unleashing the Beast*].

In Islam, there are two "houses" or groups of people on earth today; the *Dar al Islam* (The House of Islam) and everybody else - *Dar-al-Harb* (The House of War). Islamic fundamentalists believe that the "house of war" must be transformed into the "house of Islam" and this will come through *jihad* or "holy war." Therefore, unbelievers must either be beaten into submission or be killed outright. This is the sentiment that exists in present day Iran and it is growing every day among the radical Muslims living there.

Consider just a few quotes from the Koran:

"Warfare is ordained for you, though it is hateful unto you; but it may happen that you hate a thing which is good for you, and it may happen you may love a thing that is bad for you. Allah knoweth, ye know not."

- Surah 11-126

"Let the people of the Gospel judge by that which Allah hath reveled therein. Whoso judgeth not that which Allah hath revealed; such are evil doers."

- Surah 5-47

"O ye that believe. Take not the Jews and Christians for friends. They are friends one to another. He among you who taketh friends is (one) of them. Lo, Allah guideth not wrongdoing folk." - Surah 5 - 51

"O ye who believe. Choose not for friends such of those who received the Scriptures before you, and of the disbelievers, as make jest and sport of your religion. But keep your duty to Allah if ye are true." - Surah 5-57

The following passages from the Koran illustrate the desire of Muslims to fight against non Muslims.

"Then when the sacred months have passed, slay the idolaters wherever you find them, and take them (captive), and besiege them, and prepare for them each ambush." - Surah 9 - 5

"Fight against such of those who have been given the Scripture as believeth not in Allah nor the Last Day, and not that which Allah hath forbidden by His messenger, and follow not the religion of truth, until they pay the tribute readily, being brought low."

- Surah IX - 30

The purpose of sharing these with you is to demonstrate that the hatred exhibited by Haman and all of those like him resides in the pages of the Koran. It is also to show that those who espouse Islam **must** hate Israel and strive to destroy her, if for no other reason than to remain true to the religion they adhere to. It seems very probable to me that the "man of sin" will come from this region preaching his hatred for Israel because this region is already prepared to receive that message. Nevertheless, in the end the enemies of Israel will all fail for the King will save His people because He loves His bride.

Now I want to "switch gears" as they say and look at another of the lesser feasts and discover some of its secrets.

HIDDEN IN HANUKKAH

"Now it was the Feast of Dedication in Jerusalem, and it was winter. And Jesus walked in the temple, in Solomon's porch." - John 10:22-23

Theologians have taught that the four centuries between the prophecy of Malachi until John the Baptist are the "four hundred years of silence." This is to mean that during this time nothing of a spiritual nature (i.e. a word from God) happened until John began to preach "Repent for the Kingdom of Heaven is at hand" (Matthew 3:2). If, as it is taught, there was no word from the Lord then there was no prophetic anointing either.

This is not totally true. There was a significant spiritual event that occurred, but because it is considered "Jewish," most Christian theologians choose to ignore it.

The event, which occurs almost two centuries before Christ, involves the Temple in Jerusalem, an evil dictator by the name of Antiochus Epiphanes IV, and an alleged miracle.

These events gave cause for the Jews to commemorate them in an eight day festival called *Hanukkah*, or "Dedication." What makes this minor feast day so interesting to us as Christians is that Jesus obviously observed it; the passage in John is evidence of this. In fact, the passage in John is the only mention of this feast in the Bible! Furthermore, the fact that Jesus, the Light of the World, goes into the Temple during this time is a hint of the nature of this feast. I believe it is to be a picture of another future event - the rebuilding of the Temple in Jerusalem.

The First Temple was destroyed by the Babylonians in about 606 BC. That Temple was rebuilt by Nehemiah, Ezra and those returning to Israel during the Persian era, howbeit, in the midst of trouble. Eventually the Greeks overthrew the Persians under Alexander the Great. As powerful and dominating as he was, Alexander nevertheless was extremely tolerant of the Jews and their Temple practices. That changed, though, when he died in Babylon.

When he died, he left no instructions regarding his kingdom and thus, the vast Grecian empire was divided into four parts. One of those divisions was the Seleucids (Syria). From this group arose Antiochus IV, the man who would subject the Jews to cruel tyranny and in the process become a picture of the Antichrist.

Like Pharaoh and Agag, Antiochus is actually a title given to the monarchs of Syria during this era. There were actually thirteen different monarchs who ruled for close to two centuries. Antiochus Epiphanes (which means "the risen god") invaded Israel in part because of their refusal to acknowledge him or any of the other pagan gods as deity.

When he invaded Israel, he overran Jerusalem and the Temple, changing laws so that the Jew's obedience to the Law of Moses would be deemed illegal. He removed the rightful Temple priests and replaced them with Greek priests. He forbade the Temple offerings and sacrifices, the keeping of Sabbath, circumcision, and celebrating the Feasts of Israel. To add insult to injury, he sacrificed unclean animals, primarily swine, upon the holy altar. He built altars, shrines and images dedicated to Zeus with the Temple compound. As a result, many Jews fled and went into hiding. For this reason, Jewish and Christian commentators have concluded that this fulfilled certain prophecies of Daniel.

"And forces shall be mustered by him, and they shall defile the sanctuary fortress; then they shall take away the daily sacrifices, and place there abomination of desolation." - Daniel 11:31

There were devout Jews who quickly tired of this tyranny. One of them was a priest known as Mattathias. The Greek tried to compel him to sacrifice swine and when he resisted, a confrontation ensued which resulted in the death of a Greek at the hands of Mattathias. Thus began the Maccabean revolt which would eventually be led by one of Mattathias' five sons, Judah Maccabee.

According to tradition, the revolt began on the 25th of the Hebrew month *Kislev*. Three years later **to the day,** the Jews who had turned back to the Greeks, rededicated the Temple in Jerusalem. They made new doors, new curtains, rebuilt the Altar, and rekindled the Holy Menorah. In fact, the Menorah takes center stage in this story.

The main lamp - the *shamash* "servant" - of the Menorah was supposed to burn day and night. Upon removing the pollution and debris from the Temple, it was discovered that there was only one container of holy oil sufficient for just one day. According to legend, that oil lasted for eight days, just enough time until more of the holy oil could be prepared. This is why Hanukkah is also called the Festival of Lights - lights are kindled for eight nights.

So each year in late November or December (depending on the year), Jews will light a nine-branched Hanukkah menorah (eight lights for the eight days of Hanukkah and one light to represent the *shamash* or servant light). They will eat mounds of potato cakes called *latkes*. The children will compete for *gelt* (typically chocolate coins) with wooden *dreidels* (a four-sided top). On each side of the top there is inscribed a different Hebrew letter. The four different letters - נגהש *nun, gimel, hei,* and *shin* form the acrostic, נס גדול היה שם *nes gadol hayah sham* - "a great miracle happened there."

All of this activity and celebration is designed to remember what happened so long ago. What I would like to do now is examine what future events this story may allude to, namely those involving the future Temple.

THE TRIBULATION TEMPLE

For close to two-thousand years no Temple has

stood upon Mount Moriah in Jerusalem. Today, the Mosque of Omar, better known as the Dome of the Rock, sits atop the holy mountain. There are, however, certain prophecies that foretell of a future temple that will be built in Jerusalem that will factor prominently in the seven-year Tribulation.

For instance, the prophecy found in Daniel 9:27 indicates that, during this final seven year period, the Antichrist will cause "the sacrifice and oblation to cease." The "sacrifice" alludes to the sacrificial offerings at the Temple in Jerusalem. Some would suggest this was fulfilled already since no Jewish Temple exists. Notice, however that Paul speaks of the coming man of sin and says that he:

"Opposes and exalts himself above all that is called God, or that is worshiped, so that he sits as God in the temple of God, showing himself that he is God."
- 2 Thessalonians 2:4

This man who will sit in the Temple of God will also be "destroyed by brightness" by Christ's coming (2 Thessalonians 2:8). All of this is to say that, if the same person who sits in the Temple causing Temple sacrifices to cease is alive at Christ's coming, there has to be a future Temple for him to sit in. In addition to these passages, the Book of Revelation plainly states that there will indeed be a Temple in Jerusalem during the Tribulation.

"Then I was given a reed like a measuring rod. And the angel stood, saying 'Rise and measure the temple of God, the altar, and those who worship there. But leave out the court which is outside the temple, and do

not measure it; for it has been given to the Gentiles. And they will tread the holy city underfoot for forty-two months.' " - Revelation 11:1-2

If there is no Temple now, but there is one during the Tribulation, then it only makes sense that at some point before or at the beginning of the seven years, efforts to rebuild the Holy Temple will begin. After studying this for years, I am going to suggest to the reader that this Temple will be constructed in Jerusalem during the first forty-two months of the Tribulation. Here are my reasons.

Orthodox Jews believe that the prophet Elijah will reappear in the future and announce the coming of the Messiah. This, is of course, based on the prophecy in Malachi 4:5, which says:

"Behold, I will send you Elijah the prophet before the coming of the great and dreadful day of the LORD." - Malachi 4:5

Christ Himself stated that, "Elijah must first come and restore all things" (Matthew 17:11). I believe that part of this restoration will be when Elijah appears as one of the two witnesses in Revelation 11 to assist in the rebuilding of the Temple.

There is a noted professor in Jerusalem who has spent thousands of hours studying the Temple, its ancient location and the process of rebuilding the House of God. He admits that, under normal and peaceful circumstances, the process would not take that long. However, because of certain required prayers and rituals during construction and the subsequent dedication, the process would take about three-and-one-half years, or forty-two months. In fact, he suspects that when the time comes to rebuild it, the process will begin in the fall with the Temple being dedicated at the time of Passover.

This is very interesting considering that the two witnesses, one being Elijah, are empowered for forty-two months before being slain by the Beast. If the process began at the beginning of the Tribulation and concluded forty-two months later - at the midpoint of the Tribulation - the Antichrist would invade Jerusalem, kill the two witnesses, take over the entire Temple Mount and stop any Temple rituals including the sacrifice and oblation.

What does this have to do with Hanukkah? As we have learned, when this Temple is eventually erected, it will soon thereafter be polluted and defiled by another "Antiochus," the Antichrist. Like Antiochus IV, we know that the Antichrist will not only present himself as being above God, but will intentionally defile God's house by setting up an abomination that makes desolate (Daniel 11:31).

I believe that this "abomination" is the "image of the beast" spoken of in Revelation 13:15. Even though the prophecy in Daniel is thought to have been fulfilled by Antiochus IV - and it was - Christ confirms that the prophecy will be fulfilled again.

"Therefore when you see the abomination of desolation, spoken of by Daniel the prophet, standing in the holy place (whoever reads, let him understand), then let those who are in Judea flee to the mountains."
- Matthew 24:15-16

That Matthew adds a parenthetical statement - "whoever reads, let him understand" - strongly suggests that the prophecy in Daniel was thought to have been fulfilled in the First century. It *was* fulfilled and yet Christ's warning not only says the prophecy will be fulfilled again, but connects the coming Antichrist to his forerunner Antiochus IV. That means that, without a doubt, Hanukkah presents a picture of the future temple, its defilement and, ultimately the rededication of the Temple of God and the restoration of God's people. Now consider this interesting scenario.

The prophetic Scriptures give us certain numerical calculations to determine when certain things will happen. Many of these calculations center around the future Tribulation. For instance, the Bible makes sure we understand that the first forty-two months of the Tribulation are 1,260 days (Revelation 11:3, 13-5). As we have already noted, the Antichrist will kill the two witnesses, defile the Temple and set up his image to be worshiped by millions in the middle of the seven years, or after 1,260 days.

Now recall that Antiochus defiled the Temple of God and set up an abominable image in its courts. History records that for **three years**, the Temple was desecrated until it was finally cleansed and rededicated by the Maccabeans. Also recall that Daniel had predicted this would happen and centuries later Christ, quoting Daniel, predicted that it would happen again. But now look at what else Daniel had to say about this event.

"And from the time that the daily sacrifice is taken away, and the abomination of desolation is set up,

there shall be one thousand two hundred and ninety days." - Daniel 12:11

Again the first half of the Tribulation is 1,260 days. After this time, the Antichrist will kill the two witnesses. I believe that Daniel's prophecy indicates that thirty days later, he will set up the abomination that makes desolate which would account for the 1,290 days mentioned in Daniel 12:11. When the two witnesses are killed at the mid-point of the Tribulation there would still be 1,260 days remaining in the Tribulation. Now Daniel records that:

"Blessed is he who waits, and comes to the one thousand three hundred and thirty-five days."
- Daniel 12:12

This prophecy suggests the possibility that the cleansing of the Temple that has been defiled by the Antichrist may occur during Hanukkah just as it had occurred centuries before. Here is how this is possible. When Christ returns to the earth with the saints at the end of the Tribulation (Jude 14), that will mark the end of the second 1,260 day period. All the clues given in the seven biblical feasts indicate that this will be during the fall - the time of Rosh Hashana, Yom Kippur and Tabernacles.

Specifically, we understand that Christ will judge the nations on some future Yom Kippur which falls on 10 Tishri. Still, the prophecy of Daniel says the blessing is upon those who can wait until the 1,335th day. In other words, if this future Yom Kippur signals the end of the last 1,260 days, there are still seventy five days until the blessing of Daniel 12:12 is realized. Interestingly enough, beginning at Yom Kippur and counting forward seventy-five days brings us to 25 Kislev on the Hebrew calendar. That day is the first day of Hanukkah!

We understand that the next temple will be defiled by the Antichrist and that this will occur at the mid-point of the Tribulation (Revelation 13:5). He will trample down the city of Jerusalem and "make war with the saints" (Revelation 13:7) for that three and one-half years. But when Christ returns and the Antichrist, the false prophet and their demonic kingdom are destroyed, then Christ will sit upon His Throne and rule for one thousand years. Yet, there seems to be a hint that when He returns, Christ will first cleanse the Temple Mount - a process that may last seventy-five days - and rededicate His Temple during Hanukkah; a festival, by the way, that celebrates the "Light of the World."

And so, the prophecy encoded in the story of Hanukkah, like the story of Purim, paints a picture for us of those things that will occur during the seven year Tribulation and, most importantly, what the outcome will be. At the end of that time, Christ will return to save His people and cleanse the Temple of God once and for all!

Chapter Eight

SECRETS OF
THE PARABLES

According to W.E. Vines Dictionary, a parable is "placing of one thing beside another with a view to comparison. . . . It is a narrative drawn using nature, human circumstances, the object of which is to set forth a spiritual message."

Though the Bible is full of parables, the one most people are familiar with are the parables of Christ found in the Gospels. To teach in this parabolic manner was commonplace among rabbis of his day and thereafter. It was and is a way to convey deep spiritual concepts in an easy-to grasp word story. This is precisely what Christ did; He taught deep things in simple ways. But besides employing the teaching methods of the day, it was important that Jesus spoke in parables so that the words of the prophets might be fulfilled.

"I will open my mouth in a parable; I will utter

dark sayings of old, which we have heard and known, and our fathers have told us. We will not hide them from their children, telling them to the generation to come the praises of the LORD, and His strength, and His wonderful works that He has done." - Psalm 78:2-4

Scripture teaches us that this is exactly what Christ did.

"But without a parable He did not speak to them; and when they were alone He explained all things to His disciples." - Mark 4:34

By teaching in this manner, He hid spiritual wisdom from the world and revealed it to the children of God.

"Because it has been given to you to know the mysteries of the kingdom of heaven, but to them it has not been given. . . . Therefore I speak to them in parables, because seeing they do not see, and hearing they do not hear, nor do they understand." - Matthew 13:11,13

Ultimately, all of the parables Jesus taught are intended to educate believers in the mysteries concerning the Kingdom of Heaven. In my opinion, they can be divided into three main groups each dealing with the specifics of these mysteries. The primary group contains parables that teach of the end of the age and Christ's return. These parables reveal how various end time attacks will occur and of the "age to come" when the Kingdom of God will take control of all nations. Furthermore, a study of the parables will reveal deeper truths often overlooked!

THE TIMING OF CHRIST'S RETURN

Many early Christians believed that Christ would return in their day. Some even believed that it would be so soon, in fact, that John the Beloved would not die until Christ returned (John 21:20-23). By studying the parables, it becomes apparent that Christ taught that His return would occur in the distant future.

"After a long time the lord of those servants came and settled accounts with them." -Matthew 25:19

"It is like a man going to a far country, who left his house and gave authority to his servants, and to each his work, and commanded the doorkeeper to watch. Watch therefore, for you do not know when the master of the house is coming." - Mark 13:34-35

If you were to read the entirety of these parables, you would see that the attitude of people concerning His coming is revealed. Apparently, the amount of time that passed in these stories is what made the people feel the Lord was not coming. Consider this account:

"But if that evil servant says in his heart, 'My master is delaying his coming'. . . the master of that servant will come on a day when he is not looking for him and at an hour that he is not aware of."
- Matthew 24:48,50

Again, the parable infers that the Lord doesn't return immediately or as soon as the servants expect, or else they would have behaved differently. They would not have beat and mistreated their workers or ate and drank, becoming drunk (Luke 12:45). The parables tell us that "unprofitable servants" will be cut in two and appointed "his portion with the unbelievers" (Luke 12:46).

We see this in our day as well. Even though it is fast becoming apparent that we are in the end of days, still people scoff and doubt as to His coming - just as Scripture predicted.

"Knowing this first: that scoffers will come in the last days, walking according to their own lusts, and saying, 'Where is the promise of His coming? For since the fathers fell asleep, all things continue as they were from the beginning of creation.' " - 2 Peter 3:3-4

Even though the parables hinted that the Lord's return would be "far away," at least from the perspective those early believers, those same parables warned all believers to be watching lest we miss His return.

"Watch therefore, for you do not know what hour your Lord is coming." - Matthew 24:42

There are several Greek words translated as "watch." The word used in this passage *gregoreuo* means "to keep a guard watch at night." Another word, *koustodia*, means "to guard or keep watch over something." It is related to the Latin *custodia* from which we get our English word "custody." In short, Christ is telling all believers to remain spiritually and morally alert; don't get lazy and careless for He is coming when you don't expect Him.

PREPARATION PARABLES

There are four parables that speak very clearly about the need for His people to remain sober and be prepared in anticipation of His coming. The parable of the ten virgins in Matthew 25 is one of these. In the parable all ten are awaiting the bridegroom's arrival. All ten apparently knew the bride groom was returning but He had delayed his appearing. They all brought lamps and oil for their vigil and they all fell asleep. Yet, when the call came at midnight that the bridegroom was coming, five were prepared and five were not.

What was the difference? The five wise virgins had brought along an additional vessel of oil just in case the bridegroom didn't come when they thought He would. The foolish did not. When the shout came, the foolish were forced to go seeking oil - something they should have already done - and were, consequently, shut out of the wedding chamber. They missed their opportunity because they weren't prepared.

In that same chapter, Jesus gives us the parable of the three servants who were given talents or money. All the servants were given a certain amount of money to invest; one was given five talents, one was given two talents and one was given one talent. The master took a long journey but then returned to take an account of the investments. In the parable, the two servants who had been given five and two talents, respectively, doubled their investment and were praised for their accomplishments.

The last servant who had been given only one talent had done nothing, citing his master's hard nature as the reason why. But the master reveals what the real issue is - wickedness and laziness. In the end, this unprepared and unprofitable servant was cast into outer darkness. It could be argued that, not only was this servant lazy, but his wickedness was expressed by his greed. In other words, he was not willing to use the resources he had been given to invest in the furthering of the kingdom.

In Matthew 22, Christ teaches the parable of the Wedding Feast in which a certain king sent out invitations to his son's wedding. Those who were bidden were too busy to come; some even killed his servants as they delivered the invitation. So the invitation went out into the highways and hedges to compel whosoever would to come. One of those who came did not wear the proper garments and was bound and thrown out. Then Christ says:

"For many are called, but few are chosen."
- Matthew 22:14

This Scripture is understood to mean, "All are called, few choose to answer the call." Those who were first bidden did not care to answer the call and some of those who did would not wear the proper garment. In other words, they did not prepare themselves for the wedding by wearing garments of righteousness. Scripture says that the ones who are granted the privilege of coming to the Marriage Supper of the Lamb have made "themselves ready" (Revelation 19:7-8).

In all cases, the people and servants in these stories did not take the proper steps to prepare themselves spiritually and practically for the coming of the Master. The Master was then forced to expose their wickedness and lack of preparation. What should they have done?

They should have been watching and praying so that they "may be counted worthy to escape all these things that will come to pass" (Luke 21:36). They should have taken what they had been given and put it to the Master's use, whether that be finances, talents or otherwise (Matthew 25:27). They should have kept their proper garments and not defiled them so that they may walk with him "in white" (Revelation 3:4). In short, it is our responsibility to remain sober and to do what we are told to do that we may stand before The Son of Man having prepared for this encounter.

THE END TIME BATTLES

"Another parable He put forth to them, saying The kingdom of heaven is like a man who sowed good seed in his field, but while men slept, his enemy came and sowed tares among the wheat and went his way. But when the grain had sprouted and produced a crop, then the tares also appeared. So the servants of the owner came and said to him, 'Sir, did you not sow good seed in your field? How then does it have tares?' He said to them, 'An enemy hath done this.' The servants said to him, 'Do you want us then to go and gather them up?' But he said, 'No, lest while you gather up the tares you

also uproot the wheat with them. Let both grow togeth-er until the harvest, and at the time of harvest I will say to the reapers, First gather together the tares and bind them in bundles to burn them, but gather the wheat into my barn.' " - Matthew 13:24-30

Search the Scriptures and you will see that major battles have most often occurred during the time of harvest. In the Bible, the enemy would attack when the grain was about to be collected to be taken into the barns. Here are just a few examples: Samson's battles were in the time of the wheat harvest (Judges 15:1); Gideon's battles occurred in the time of the wheat harvest (Judges 6:11); David's bat-tles were centered around the harvest time (2 Samuel 4:6); Rizpa lost her sons during the barley harvest (2 Samuel 21:9).

Likewise, end time battles will occur at the time of harvest, which, according to Christ, is at the end of the age (Matthew 13:39). In many of the parables, and especially in the parable of the wheat and tares, the harvest deals with gathering souls into the kingdom.

"But when the grain ripens, immediately he puts in the sickle because the harvest has come." - Mark 4:29

Because of what harvest represents, this is also the time when the Adversary, the Devil, is most likely to strike. In the "Wheat and Tare" parable, we see that the enemy actually tried to undermine the harvest beforehand by sow-ing a poisonous seed in the field.

Biblically speaking, the tares, also called *darnel* in

many translations, come from the Greek *zizanion*, which is actually believed to be a transliteration of the Hebrew זונים *zunim*. According to commentator David H.Stern, *zunim* is a poisonous rye grass that looks like wheat until the heads appear. According to Judaism, *zunim* is actually a degenerate form of wheat whose origins are traced to the Flood.

Here is the point, the tare is not compatible with the wheat and, so as both these seeds grow, they are bound to fight with one another over the same water, the same nutrients and the same patch of ground. This battle continues until the "time of the harvest." At that time, the reapers will destroy the seed that the Devil has sown. Still, and this is the point, the struggle continues right up until that time. Therefore, as harvest - the end of the age - approaches, we should not be surprised when attacks from the enemy come and battles break out.

Not only that, but this parable teaches us that the tares are **among** the wheat. In other words, they live in the same field that the wheat does. This says to me that many of the battles we will face in the end times will come from our own churches, even our own families - the good live among the bad. Consider the parable of the dragnet.

"Again, the kingdom of heaven is like a dragnet that was cast into the sea and gathered some of every kind, which, when it was full, they drew to shore, and they sat down and gathered the good into vessels, but threw the bad away. So it will be at the end of the age. The angels will come forth, separate the wicked from among the just, and cast them into the furnace of fire."
- Matthew 13:47-50

When the net is full - which speaks of harvest - all types of fish are pulled in. That means that good and bad, clean and unclean or kosher and non-kosher are gathered in the same net. In other words, the net doesn't distinguish between clean and unclean, it is those who have been given the job of sifting through the catch who make this determination. In the meantime clean fish and unclean fish swim in the same pool of waters.

Such is our situation here on earth. We are living among the unjust and so we should expect that as the net goes forth to gather the harvest, battles will break out as Satan tries to retain control and undermine God's Plan. Even so, keep in mind that, in many of the parables that hint at battles and loss (e.g. Luke 15), the story ends with those who have suffered rejoicing!

ENCODED PARABLES

Besides the profound messages about life in general or the warnings to stay prepared for the end of days, there are parables which also have something unique hidden within them. This hidden element is especially true when it comes to those of us who live in the West and who do not understand the Hebrew language or culture. In other words, many times Jesus says something that doesn't make sense to us, but made perfect sense to those living at that time. Still, there are those things that were hidden from everyone until it was time to understand them.

In addition to the many parables, this hidden element also shows up in different events that occurred in the life of Jesus. For instance, after the Resurrection, Peter decided to return to fishing in the Galilee. On one particular morning, after fishing all night and catching nothing, the disciples spy a man they eventually recognize as being Jesus. They were able to discern His identity after He has commanded them to, "Cast the net on the right side of the boat and you will find some" (John 21:6). When they complied their empty net was filled and they knew the man was the Lord. When the bulging net was dragged to shore, the disciples counted a total of 153 fish; why 153?

One theory is based on the notion that "153" is an important value in Hebrew thought. It is important because of the phrase, "I am the LORD your God." This phrase appears many times in Scripture, one of the most notable instances being found in Isaiah.

"For I am the LORD your God, the Holy One of Israel, your Savior . . . Fear not for I am with you. I will bring your descendants from the east, and gather you from the west. I will say to the north, 'Give them up!' And to the south, 'Do not keep them back!' Bring My sons from afar, and My daughters from the ends of the earth." - Isaiah 43:3, 5-6

This passage is a prophecy of how, in the end of days, God will gather all of His people from the ends of the earth and bring them into their inheritance. Keep in mind that the disciples had been called to be "fishers of men" (Matthew 4:9) and many times in Scripture, including an example in Isaiah, the seas are used to personify the nations or the gentiles - that is where the fish are!

In this passage the Hebrew phrase "I am the LORD

your God" is אני יהוה אלהיך *ani YHVH eloheicha.* So how is the value 153 associated with this phrase? Because ancient civilizations did not have Arabic numerals (i.e. 0, 1, 2, 3, etc.), letters were also used to express values. In Hebrew this is called "gematria." By substituting the numerical equivalents for each of the Hebrew letters in the above phrase, the sum of this phrase is 153. In other words, when reading the Torah and Prophets many Hebrews would see the phrase "I am the LORD your God." as being equivalent to 153.

When the disciples - the fishers of men - saw that they had removed 153 fish from the seas, they knew the One who had commanded and authorized them was the LORD Himself. It seems, then, that this catch of fish is symbolic of going into the nations and finding those that belong to Him. Interestingly enough, in the early 20th century, there were about one hundred nations in the world. After World War II many nations were divided and other nations formed so that by the close of the 1980s there were reportedly 153 nations in the world.

If there is a connection between this and the 153 fish, then the fact that the net was full hints, perhaps, at the "fullness" of the Gentiles (Roman 11:25). If that is so, then this story in John's gospel has an encoded message concerning the end times; that is, when you see 153 nations in the world, then you will know that the time of the fullness of the Gentiles is at hand. When that time comes, then soon "all Israel shall be saved." (Romans 11:26).

Another interpretation of the significance of the 153 fish comes to us from one of the early Christian fathers, St. Augustine. In his opinion the number 100 alludes to the fulness of the Gentiles (Genesis 15:13), the number 50 alludes to the fullness of Israel (Leviticus 23) and the number 3 alludes to the Godhead (1 John 5:7). Therefore, the number 153 would allude to fullness or completion.

There is another link between Christ and the number 153 and this one involves the Greek alphabet. Like Hebrew, the Greek letters can be interchanged for numbers. The three Greek letters IXO, which are an early abbreviation of ICHTUS, form an acrostic, "Jesus Christ God's Son and Savior." These letters in Greek total 153. Therefore the 153 fish would be a hidden allusion that Jesus Christ was truly the son of God.

Are all of these points of interest only strange coincidences, or a deeper meaning that must be researched? If we believe and understand the concept of how stories can hold keys to deeper understanding, then these things are possible.

There are many other parables that Jesus taught and many other messages contained within, but all of them lead to this conclusion - all His people shall be saved! To address all of the parables would be close to impossible, but I have tried to give the reader a good idea of how Jesus' parables, as well as other notable events in Scripture, are there to paint a picture of the end of days. Now, there is one more issue I wish to discuss and that is the final climactic battle before the kingdoms of this world become the kingdoms of our God and of His Christ.

Chapter Nine

THE ARMAGEDDON CODE

"That which has been is what will be; that which is done is what will be done, and there is nothing new under the sun." - Ecclesiastes 1:9

"That which is has already been, and what is to be has already been; and God requires an account of what is past." - Ecclesiastes 3:15

With all the prophecies fulfilled in the last century, even in our lifetime, there are still major prophecies that remain unfulfilled. As we begin this chapter, I want to deal with two predictions that have not happened, but are clearly on the horizon. The prophecies I am referring to deal with two Middle Eastern cities that are set for future destruction - Gaza and Damascus.

The Prophet Isaiah predicted in specific terms that, in the future, many nations would see destruction. Here are a few.

- Babylon (Isaiah 13).
- Moab or Jordan (Isaiah 15).
- Damascus or Syria (Isaiah 17).
- The land beyond Ethiopia (Isaiah 18).
- Egypt (Isaiah 18).
- Arabia (Isaiah 21).

As I said, he made specific predictions about these nations. For example, he says of Egypt that this nation will experience bitter infighting, civil war perhaps: "Egyptian will fight against Egyptian" (Isaiah 19:2). Isaiah speaks in concert with other prophecies all of which further predict that Egypt will ultimately be conquered and suffer intense natural disasters (Isaiah 19:4-5; Daniel 11:40-45; Revelation 16:12).

The point here is to show just how specific these prophecies are and how other prophecies complement what Isaiah saw and wrote. That being said, I want to look at the specifics of another Isaiah prophecy, one dealing with the future of the city of Damascus.

THE DEATH OF DAMASCUS

"The burden against Damascus. Behold Damascus will cease from being a city, and it will be a ruinous heap. The cities of Aroer are forsaken. They will be for flocks, which lie down, and no one will make them afraid. The fortress also will cease from Ephraim, the

kingdom from Damascus, and the remnant of Syria; They will be as the glory of the children of Israel, saith the LORD of hosts." - Isaiah 17:1-3

At about 4,000 years old, Damascus is one of the oldest cities in the world, if not the oldest. Its ancient history dates back at least to the time of Abraham and is mentioned in Genesis 14:15.

"Among ancient cities of the world, Damascus is perhaps the oldest continuously inhabited. Its name, *Dimashq* in Arabic . . . derives from *dimashka*, a word of pre-Semitic origin suggesting that the beginning of Damascus goes back to a time before recorded history"
- Encyclopedia Britannica

It is believed to have been settled because it was a desert oasis making it extremely valuable to all those who made their way to the Syrian capital. Still, through the years it has been attacked, its vineyards and orchards destroyed, but always spared total destruction. And despite being in the middle of several wars with Israel, miraculously, it has continued as a city to this day. The Bible predicts, however, that Damascus' days are numbered. Why and how will this destruction occur?

When you consider how the destruction of Damascus affects other regions, the "why" starts to come into focus. The prophecy points out that the ramifications of Damascus' downfall will also bring an end to "Aroer" and the "fortress of Ephraim." Aroer is found in what is now south central Jordan. The fortress of Ephraim, I believe, is referring to lands in Israel that were deeded to Ephraim the son of Joseph. These lands are now referred to by most of the world as the West Bank. So it seems that whatever conflagration destroys Damascus will also affect a part of Jordan and the West Bank.

In the end, Damascus will be no more and those who had heretofore controlled parts of Jordan and the West Bank will be conquered if not destroyed themselves. In short, this sounds like the war that brings an end to the so-called "Israeli-Palestinian" conflict. The strong inference here is that Israel will be the victor but at a great price (Isaiah 17:4-9). The cost to Israel will be that only a remnant will remain after the destruction! Obviously, Isaiah is describing a cataclysmic event that will, no doubt, reverberate around the world causing nations to be in an uproar and, eventually, attempting to force "peace" upon the region.

"Woe to the multitude of people, who make a noise like the roar of the seas, and to the rushing of nations, that make a rushing like the rushing of mighty waters! The nations will rush like the rushing of many waters; but God will rebuke them and they will flee far away, and be chased like the chaff of the mountains before the wind; like a rolling thing before the whirlwind. Then behold, at eventide, trouble! And before the morning, he is no more. This is the portion of those who plunder us, and the lot of those who rob us."

- Isaiah 17:12-14

A war that destroys Syria, adversely affects the current status of the West Bank and parts of Jordan, and causes nations to attempt to plunder Israel sounds like the logical outcome of the current political and military situation evolving in the Middle East. The truly interesting part of this is what transpires afterwards when nations come rushing in to rob and plunder Israel. Isaiah says that they will be destroyed - in the evening! So, not only will there be a war that destroys Syria, but this apparently incites another war just as destructive, if not more so.

Moreover, I am of the opinion that what Isaiah describes as the result of Damascus' destruction (the nations rushing as many waters) sounds very similar to what Ezekiel described in chapters 38 and 39 of his book - the war of Gog and Magog. Consider that Ezekiel describes an invasion of forces from the north who:

- Come like a cloud covering the land (38:9)
- Come to take a plunder (38:12)

When Gog and his confederation invade Israel, the Scripture says that Israel is dwelling "safely" (Ezekiel 38:8), something they do not currently enjoy with the current situation. Furthermore, at the time of the invasion, they dwell safely in a land of "unwalled villages" (Ezekiel 38:11). In an effort to protect its citizens from terrorists who would cross from Gaza and the West Bank into Israel, the nation is currently constructing a wall to separate Israel from the so-called West Bank. If there was a decisive war that changed the status quo in the West Bank, there would be no need for a wall - "all of them dwelling without walls"

(Ezekiel 38:11) - but would incite many nations against them.

When Gog comes into the land, God says that He will turn them back with sudden and horrific destruction (Ezekiel 38:22, 39:6). Gog's armies will fall on the mountains of Israel (Ezekiel 39:4) and will be buried in the "valley of the passengers on the east of the sea" (Ezekiel 39:11). This particular passage is fascinating when you consider how it reads in the Hebrew text. The phrase "valley of the passengers" is גי העברים *gai ha abarim* - the Abarim valley.

Look on a map and you will see that the Abarim mountains and the Abarim valley lie just east of the Dead Sea in present day Jordan! But Ezekiel says this valley burial ground will be in Israel. The only way I can see for this prophecy to occur as described would mean, before Gog's armies invade the mountains of Israel, there would have been a prior war in which the West Bank and parts of Jordan came under Israeli control. Isaiah's prophecy said that the cities of Aroer (part of Jordan) would be forsaken!

You must also consider that Gog's armies are confident that they will be able to come and take a spoil. Is it because the war with Damascus and others has left the Israelis weakened? Remember, this is what Isaiah described. Not only that, but look at the roster of nations who invade Israel in Ezekiel's prophecy and you will notice that Syria is not mentioned. Is it because she is no more? In the end, God's people will "have respect for the Holy One of Israel" (Isaiah 17:7) and His name will be known "in the midst of My people . . . then the nations shall know that I am the LORD, the Holy One of Israel" (Ezekiel 39:7).

THE WMD FACTOR

In my opinion, an Israeli war with Syria and other terror groups such as *Hezbollah* and *Hamas* could be the explosion that ignites the entire Middle Eastern powder keg. The total annihilation of Damascus hints that Israel may employ non-conventional weapons which would, of course, provoke other hostile nations to retaliate. But what is the spark that lights the fuse?

First, it should be noted that both Hamas and Hezbollah receive instructions and support from Damascus. Not only that, but the leaders of both organizations reside in Damascus and from there make threats against Israel. Couple this with the fact that Syria's leadership would love nothing more than to be the state that accomplishes what a vast confederation of Muslim states have been unable to do so far - destroy Israel once and for all, but how?

Recently, a Syrian reporter living in France leaked information concerning an alleged cache of weapons of mass destruction (WMDs) inside of Syria. According to the reporter, a friend in Syrian intelligence told him precisely where the weapons were buried. Supposedly, these WMDs are located in three subterranean sites in Syria. They were allegedly purchased by the Syrian Defense Minister for fifty million dollars - but from whom?

Ali Ibrahim al Tikriti, the Southern regional commander for Saddam Hussein, oversaw vast amounts of Iraqi chemical and biological weapons. Al Tikriti defected in 1991 and subsequently verified that Saddam did, in fact, have a moderate arsenal of WMDs.

An Iraqi known as George Sada was once one of

Saddam's top two Air Force officers. He has stated that these weapons were moved to Syria six weeks before the second Gulf War began. He claims that two Iraqi Airways Boeing jets were converted into cargo planes. Posing as regularly scheduled commercial flights, these planes flew undetected into Syria and delivered these weapons to the Syrians. In all, Sada said it took fifty-six flights to accomplish this, but that they were all relocated.

Not too long ago, the Kingdom of Jordan supposedly seized twenty tons of dangerous chemicals from al Qaeda operatives. The cargo included VX, Sarin and seventy other types of chemicals that had the potential to kill as many as 80,000 people. The report stated that the deadly contraband was being transported by trucks and that the trucks had originated in Syria. Amazingly, the media said very little.

Here is the point: no significant amounts of WMDs were found in Iraq, much to the dismay of the Bush Administration and the U.S., for that matter. Yet, intelligence sources were convinced that the offending material was there before the war. Where did it all go? All roads seem to lead to Syria. If Saddam's WMDs did end up in Syria, what might Bashar Assad and his henchmen do with it? Is it possible that the Syrian despots might release some of these weapons to groups such as *Hezbollah* or *Hamas*? Would these groups use these types of weapons against the Israelis? One thing is for sure; if they did use them, Israel would retaliate in overwhelming force.

THE GAZA PROPHECY

While the rank and file of *Hezbollah's* armies are concentrated in Lebanon, *Hamas'* militias are centered primarily in the Gaza strip. This is the area that was once home to the ancient Philistines!

The people who are today called Palestinians claim that their heritage goes back to these ancient people, who were constant antagonists where Israel was concerned. Frankly, their ancestry is a matter of debate but what is crystal clear is that these people are demanding a sovereign state of their own, presumably to be called "Palestine," with its capital being east Jerusalem.

Scripture does refer to "Palestine" by name in about ten different passages, but seldom in a positive way. Here are a couple of examples.

"Indeed, what have you to do with Me, O Tyre and Sidon, and all the coasts of Philistia (Palestine)? Will you retaliate against Me? But if you retaliate against Me, swiftly and speedily I will return your retaliation upon your own head." - Joel 3:4

I should point out here that the context of this passage in Joel addresses those who seek to part or divide the land of Israel and cast lots for His people (Joel 3:2-3)

"Do not rejoice, all of you of Philistia (Palestine) because the rod that struck you is broken: For out of the serpent's root will come forth a viper, and its offspring will be a fiery flying serpent. The firstborn of the poor

will feed, and needy will lie down in safety; I will kill your roots with famine, and it will slay your remnant. Wail, O gate! Cry, O city! All you of Philistia are dissolved, for smoke will come from the north, and no one will be alone in his appointed times. What will they answer the messengers of the nation? That the LORD has founded Zion, and the poor of his people shall take refuge in it." - Isaiah 14:29-32

The point is, at least as far as these two verses are concerned, Philistia or Palestine will be destroyed at some point in the future. If Philistia is to be understood as the ancient abode of the Philistines, then the area now called the Gaza strip is set for future destruction. Considering that this is the region that spawned and currently houses the terror group *Hamas*, it is not too difficult to understand why that might happen. Furthermore, I think it is interesting that no Israelis live there anymore - they were forcibly removed from the area.

Keep in mind what we have learned about the destruction of Damascus and the reverberations that will be felt around the world. Remember that when Damascus is destroyed, parts of Jordan and the entire West Bank will be vanquished by Israel. With that in mind, look at what Amos has to say concerning Damascus or Gaza.

"For three transgressions of Damascus, and for four, I will not turn away its punishment, . . . I will also break the gate bar of Damascus, . . . For three transgressions of Gaza, and for four, I will not turn away its punishment; because they took captive the whole cap-

tivity to deliver them up to Edom. But I will send a fire
upon the wall of Gaza, which shall devour its palaces....
and the remnant of the Philistines shall perish, says the
Lord GOD." - Amos 1:3, 5-8

In other words Amos predicts that, not only will
Damascus be destroyed, but joining her will be Gaza. In
fact, not just Gaza but Tyre, Edom and parts of Jordan
(Amos 1:9-15). Therefore, it seems to me that the fire that
comes upon "the wall of Gaza" also falls, maybe simulta-
neously, upon Damascus and her puppet state Lebanon
(Tyre), upon the West Bank (Edom) and parts of Jordan
(Ammon). This certainly seems to agree with the scenario
that Isaiah's prophecy presents.

There are other prophecies concerning the Gaza
Strip's future that makes a clear statement: there are those
who live in that region who have provoked the Holy One of
Israel.

"For Gaza shall be forsaken and Ashkelon desolate." - Zephaniah 2:4

"Ashkelon shall see it and fear, Gaza also shall be
very sorrowful, . . . the king shall perish from Gaza."
- Zechariah 9:5

I will ask the same question that I asked concerning
Damascus: Why and how does the destruction come? Once
again "why" seems obvious to me. The fanatics in Gaza,
those who comprise the ranks of *Hamas* and similar terror
groups will stop at nothing when it comes to destroying the

Israelis. They are perfectly willing to use themselves and their children as weapons to murder noncombatants, including women and children. Thus far their tactics have killed dozens at one time, but what happens if they decide to use other types of weapons that are far more destructive? Let me put it this way.

If Damascus has WMDs and the leadership of *Hamas* is in Damascus, isn't it just a matter of time before *Hamas* operatives are given these weapons to carry out murderous attacks that can yield far more Israeli deaths? If that happens and the source of these weapons is connected to Syria and other neighboring accomplices, what might Israel be forced to do? In my opinion, the stage is being set now for the next major war and by that I do not mean the war of Gog and Magog. I believe that another will precede that one and this next war will further cement Jerusalem as the "burdensome stone" in the eyes of the world (Zechariah 12:2-3).

This may explain "why," but "how" does it come about? Again, it seems Israel may be forced to respond in a very determined and very destructive way, perhaps even using non-conventional weapons. If this were to occur, then imagine what the world's response would be. There would be some like the United Nations who would try to enforce sanctions upon Israel until they surrendered their weapons and conquered territories. When that failed, there would be those who would undertake military action to seize Israel's WMDs (Ezekiel 38 & 39), maybe using George Bush's reasons for going into Iraq as their justification for going into Israel.

In the end this is what becomes obvious; this will

set the stage for the Antichrist and ultimately Armageddon. Going back to the prophecy in Isaiah 14 concerning Philistia we see that when Palestine is broken, not to mention Damascus and other nearby enemies, something deadly arises from the ashes of the destruction.

"For out of the serpent's root will come forth a viper, and its offspring will be a fiery flying serpent."
- Isaiah 14:29

To put it into plain language, when this war concludes, soon after a viper will come onto the scene and give birth to a "flying fiery serpent." It is interesting that this description closely resembles the emblem of the PLO. But even more interesting is what Scripture says will occur at the end of days.

"And another sign appeared in heaven: behold, a great fiery red dragon having seven heads and ten horns, and seven diadems on his heads."
- Revelation 12:3

This red or "flame colored" dragon (better rendered "serpent") is mentioned thirteen times in the book of Revelation. This is the beast that will arise just before Christ returns to sit upon His Throne in Jerusalem. It appears that the Beast is given opportunity to arise because of the continual state of war in the Middle East, not to mention that many of the nations who are currently dominant powers will be reduced to almost nothing. These wars will create a vast power vacuum in the region giving the

Antichrist the convenience of walking onto a political stage that has been cleared of the significant obstacles. Consequently, the table will be set for the last great battle the world knows as Armageddon.

GIDEON AND ARMAGEDDON

"And they gathered them together to the place called in Hebrew, Armageddon." - Revelation 16:16

After the Antichrist seizes power and creates unprecedented, global chaos for forty-two months, humanity will enter the last conflict and finally stand at the precipice of total annihilation. As the armies of the world prepare to march on Jerusalem, they will gather in a 200 square mile valley at the foot of a hill called *Har Megiddon*. This valley is commonly referred to in Scripture (over thirty times) as the valley of Jezreel, which means "God will sow."

The history of this valley is synonymous with agriculture and, unfortunately, war and bloodshed. It is fair to say that most of the ancient military powers have fought here. The reason for that is due to its strategic location; it is the crossroad of the Levant, the fertile crescent that stretches from Egypt to Mesopotamia. In the ancient world, if Egypt wanted to invade Syria or if Babylon wanted to invade Egypt, all roads led through this valley. Consequently the valley has been saturated with the blood of thousands.

One example of this bloody history is found in the book of Judges and the story of Gideon. As the story begins, the Midianites - people from the Arabian peninsula - had invaded Israel with no one willing to resist them. Consequently, they oppressed the Israelis for seven years (Judges 6:1).

We are told that, at the time of the threshing of wheat, God sent an angel to a man named Gideon (Judges 6:11). I should remind you here that, attacks almost always come during the time of harvest and, according to the parable of the wheat and tares, the harvest represents the end of the age (Matthew 13).

When the wheat is gathered in to be threshed, the tool that is used is called, in Latin, a *tribulim*. This tool is used to crush the grain, more specifically, the hard and unfruitful exterior of the grain called chaff. Once the chaff is broken off, the grain and chaff will be sifted so that the chaff can be removed and discarded, typically by burning it. That is interesting in and of itself but don't miss this point: the tool that is used - the *tribulim* - is the source of the word "tribulation."

At the end of the seven-year Tribulation, or at the end of the "threshing" if you will, the final battle will occur. It was after seven years of oppression that the Angel of the Lord appeared to Gideon to call him to war on behalf of Israel.

When we study the details of this story, we see that also during this time, the Amalekites and the **people of the East** would come up against Israel as well (Judges 6:3). In Revelation, we see that the "kings of the east" will come up to the final battle (Revelation 16:12, 14); a battle that will be joined by all nations (Zechariah 14:2).

Just before the climactic battle that Gideon was

called to lead, Scripture says that the Midianites, the Amalekites and the people of the East gathered together and encamped in the "Valley of Jezreel" (Judges 6:33) or as we know it, the Valley of Armageddon.

According to the account, immediately after this, the Spirit of God came upon Gideon who then blew "the trumpet" or the shofar to assemble the people of Israel (Judges 6:34). In the end, his army of thousands was weeded out until there were only three hundred remaining - a remnant.

Just before the valiant three hundred were to strike the Midianites, God told Gideon to go with his servant to the camp of his enemies. There he heard one of the Midianites tell of a disturbing dream. In the dream the enemy saw a barley cake come into camp, strike a tent and overturn it. Amazingly, the enemy interpreted this to mean that the sword of Gideon would strike and that Midian was to be delivered into his hand (Judges 7:13-14).

Barley speaks of Passover and Passover speaks of the Lamb of God. We know from Scripture that it is He who will come against all the enemies who will assemble against Israel and He will destroy them!

When Gideon and his men blew the shofar and broke the pitchers and shouted, the entire enemy camp fled in confusion, killing their own comrades as they scattered. Eventually two Midianite princes, Oreb and Zeeb, were captured and slain (Judges 7:25). "Oreb" and "Zeeb" (pronounced "ze-eb") mean "a raven" and "a wolf" respectively. In other words, these two princes paint a picture of two beasts being captured and then destroyed. Notice what happens when Christ returns.

"The beast was captured, and with him the false prophet who worked signs in his presence, by which he deceived those who received the mark of the beast, and those who worshiped his image. These two were cast alive into the lake of fire burning with brimstone."

- Revelation 19:20

I need to also point out that Zeeb was slain at the winepress (Judges 7:25). In Scripture, the winepress typically indicates war, battle and most importantly, the winepress of God's wrath.

"And he cried with a loud cry to him who had the sharp sickle, saying, 'Thrust in your sharp sickle and gather the clusters of the vine of the earth, for her grapes are fully ripe.' So the angel thrust his sickle into the earth and gathered the vine of the earth, and threw it into the great winepress of the wrath of God. And the winepress was trampled outside the city, and blood came out of the winepress, up to the horses' bridles, for one thousand six hundred furlongs."

- Revelation 14:18-20

It is the Deliverer Christ who will destroy the enemies of Israel and who will trample out the winepress.

"Now out of His mouth goes a sharp sword, that with it He should strike the nations. And He Himself will rule them with a rod of iron. He Himself treads the winepress of the fierceness and wrath of Almighty God." - Revelation 19:15

After the deaths of Oreb and Zeeb, Gideon crossed over the Jordan and traveled to Sukkot (Judges 8:5-6). Sukkot, you may remember, is the Hebrew word that is translated "tabernacles." This is the Hebrew term used for the Feast of Tabernacles, which is the last feast of Israel. Recall that this feast comes just after Yom Kippur - the day God determines who lives and dies - and Rosh Hashana, the feast of Trumpets - the Resurrection of the dead.

Sukkot is the picture of the Messianic Kingdom, when all of God's enemies have become his footstool. Before He sits upon His throne, He will tread down His enemies and will rule them with a rod of iron (Revelation 19:15). In Gideon's story, the Bible records that he "tore the flesh" of those who resisted him (Judges 8:7) and ultimately destroyed the army of the Ishmaelites, those who had survived the first battle (Judges 8:12, 24).

That Gideon's opponents were Amalekites (descendants of Esau and ancestors of Haman the Agagite), Midianites and Ishmaelites (these two groups being the ancestors of the Arab peoples) is significant, especially when it comes to the Ishmaelites. The reason is because the Bible has a lot to say about these groups at the end of the age.

ISHMAEL AT THE END

"He shall be a wild man; His hand shall be against every man, and every man's hand against him. And he shall dwell in the presence of all his brethren."
- Genesis 16:12

Those who attacked Israel in Gideon's day were, by and large, the ancestors of the Arab peoples. This is an extremely important aspect of this picture. In other words, if Gideon's story is encoded with the events of Armageddon then, at the end, the sons of Ishmael will again rise up to destroy the sons of Israel. All the clues in the story seem to point to the radical Muslims who today strive to destroy Israel and those who align themselves with the sons of Jacob.

For instance, the Bible says that, after they had slain the Ishmaelites, Gideon's men took the ornament from around the camel's necks (Judges 8:21). The word that is translated as "ornaments" is, in Hebrew, a word to denote something round "like the moon." Most everyone knows that the crescent moon is the emblem of Islam.

One of the two kings that Gideon killed just after the first battle was called Oreb. Actually it would be better rendered Orev. The interesting thing about his name, however, is its meaning and what other Hebrew words it is related to. You see, עוֹרֵב *Orev* comes from the Hebrew root word עֲרָב *arav* or as we would say, "Arab." So do you really believe that the events that are transpiring around the world are just happenstance and that prophecy is not being fulfilled? The Bible is being fulfilled before our very eyes!

The final revelation that can be gleaned from this story is that, when the battle is over, Gideon tells the people of Israel:

"The LORD shall rule over you." - Judges 8:23

When Christ has destroyed His enemies and the battle is over, He will rule and reign for one thousand years and the earth will experience something it has not known since before the fall of man - Shalom, Peace! Thus, it will be as it was in the days of Gideon when:

"The country was quiet." - Judges 8:28

Chapter Ten

WHERE ARE WE PROPHETICALLY?

During the first appearance of Christ, He fulfilled the three spring feasts. He was crucified at Passover, placed in the tomb during Unleavened Bread, and showed Himself to be alive to His disciples toward the conclusion of First Fruits (John 20:26-27). Fifty days later on the day of Pentecost, the Holy Spirit fell upon 120 believers and over 3,000 souls were converted to Christ (Acts 1:15, 2:1-4; 2:41). The gift of the Holy Spirit is promised to all believers until the very time that Christ returns (1 Corinthians 1:7). This means that, prophetically, the church is continually living at the Feast of Pentecost.

Like the apostle Peter, we are preaching salvation and the infilling of the Spirit to those who believe (Acts 2). But if we are currently at Pentecost, where are we going? What is the order of events as we move from Pentecost toward the fall feasts?

On the Jewish calendar the next major feast that follows Pentecost is Rosh Hashana, or the Feast of Trumpets. This feast is one of the "candidates" that many prophetic scholars believe the Resurrection of the dead in Christ could occur on. While there is some degree of speculation concerning this, there is an abundant supply of prophetic evidence from both the Scripture and Jewish tradition that Rosh Hashana will be the time.

Because no other major prophetic event has occurred on a fall feast day and the Return of Christ is the next main event, we can apply this to the following concept: the church has been "living at the Feast of Pentecost" for the last 1,975 years! We have been in the "dispensation of the grace of God" (Ephesians 3:2), also recognized by some scholars as, "The Church Age." The question becomes, where are we prophetically as we head toward the fall feasts, or the Rapture of the church? Are there any Hebraic prophecy parallels between Pentecost and Trumpets that would indicate what will transpire before the Rapture occurs?

THE FOUR MONTH "GAP"

Pentecost falls on the Jewish calendar, fifty days after the first Sabbath of Passover. In Christ's day, the Spirit came when the "day of Pentecost was fully come" (Acts 2:1). This means the fiftieth day had arrived in Jerusalem and the celebration was beginning at the Temple. Once Pentecost concludes, there is approximately a four month gap until the seventh month, when the fall feasts are celebrated. In the Bible there is an unusual event that occurred on the Jewish calendar between Pentecost and the Feast of

Trumpets. As previously stated, Moses received the law on Mount Sinai and presented it to the people on Pentecost. For forty days he was alone with God as God revealed his law for Israel to the prophet.

When Moses came off the mountain the Israelites were worshiping the golden calf (Exodus 32:19). In anger, Moses broke the tablets containing the Ten Commandments. Three thousand Israelites were slain (Exodus 32:28). Moses immediately ascended to the top of the mountain to intercede on behalf of Israel (Exodus 32:30). Moses repented on behalf of the people, spending a second forty day period on the mountain with God (Exodus 34:28). This second forty day period would be recognized centuries later as the season of *Teshuvah*, a Hebrew word for repentance.

THE SEASONS OF REPENTANCE

This special season is recognized each year by Jews around the world. It begins on the first of Elul which is the twelfth month on the Jewish secular (not religious) calendar. It is the last month before the Jewish New Year, called Rosh Hashana, the Feast of Trumpets. During the twenty nine days of Elul each person is to search their heart and repent. Letters are written to friends and relatives wishing them a good New Year and a good outcome on the Day of Atonement. Often the letter will conclude with the words, "May you be inscribed in the book of life." Beginning the first day of Elul, Psalms 22 is recited two times a day, from 1 Elul to 22 Tishri - or for 51 straight days!

When Elul concludes, Rosh Hashana, or Trumpets

begins. This initiates the New Year on the Jewish calendar. For ten days it is believed that the door of heaven is open to receive the prayers of the people. Finally, the season of Teshuvah climaxes and concludes on the Day of Atonement, the tenth day of Tishri. From the first of Elul to the Day of Atonement is a forty day period.

It is interesting that, prior to the blowing of the trumpets on Rosh Hashana, there is a major season of repenting in preparing of the fall feasts. The church is living between Pentecost and Trumpets! As we come closer to the Rapture when the great trumpet sounds, I believe there will be a major emphasis on repenting and turning to God! This is clear from Acts 3:19-21.

"Repent therefore and be converted, that your sins may be blotted out, so that times of refreshing may come from the presence of the Lord, and that He may send Jesus Christ, who was preached to you before, whom heaven must receive until the times of restoration of all things, which God has spoken by the mouth of all His holy prophets since the world began." - Acts 3:19-21

According to the Apostle Peter, repentance leads to a refreshing which is a part of the "restoration of all things" and that eventually leads to the return of Christ. As the church age comes to a climax and the gospel is preached around the world, there must be a call to repent, just as the season of Teshuvah is a call to repentance that leads up to the Feast of Trumpets.

FOUR MONTHS

Another interesting aspect of the four months between Pentecost and Trumpets concerns a dry season. According to the prophetic Scriptures, there will be a final outpouring of the Holy Spirit in the last days. Joel stated:

"And it shall come to pass afterward that I will pour out My Spirit on all flesh; your sons and daughters shall prophesy, your old men shall dream dreams, your young men shall see visions. And also on My menservants and on My maidservants I will pour out My Spirit in those days." - Joel 2:28-29

This outpouring is identified as the early and latter rain.

"Therefore be patient, brethren, until the coming of the Lord. See how the farmer waits for the precious fruit of the earth, waiting patiently for it until it receives the early and latter rain. You also be patient. Establish your hearts, for the coming of the Lord is at hand.
- James 5:7-8

The early and latter rains come in the fall months and in the spring months. One rain occurs as the seed is being planted in the ground and the second wave of rain falls during the early spring months. These rains prepare the soil and assist in the growth of the barley and the wheat. The barley is harvested around Passover and the wheat harvest is celebrated at Pentecost.

From a prophetic perspective the early and the latter rain would allude to two major outpourings of the Holy Spirit on earth. The first occurred in Acts 2 on the day of Pentecost. This initial outpouring of the Spirit birthed the church and continued until the time of the destruction of the Temple in 70 AD. Historically there will be a final out-pouring of the spirit "in the last days." It appears this out-pouring is occurring now, as millions of believers from all denominations are being baptized with the Holy Spirit (Acts 1:5). This final outpouring will be unleashed among the sons and daughters, upon the younger generation of believers.

THE "NO RAIN" THEOLOGY

Being a fourth generation minister from a Full Gospel background, I was taught from a child to believe in the Holy Spirit. Growing up I observed my father praying in the Spirit (in other tongues). Growing up I also heard of many Christians from other denominations who taught that the gifts of the Spirit (1 Corinthians 12) had ceased in the first century. These ill-informed church members taught that people such as my father were either deceived or satan-ically inspired. They taught that the first and last outpour-ing of the Holy Spirit was exclusively on the day of Pentecost, to assist in starting the Christian church. They taught that after the death of the original twelve apostles the manifestations of the Holy Spirit ceased.

Often they point out that, after the New Testament was completed between the third and fourth century, the miraculous gifts ceased in the church. From their point of view any person who claims to have received an infilling of the Spirit is deceived, delusional or demon possessed! Despite the fact that the Bible predicts there would be an early and latter rain before the return of Christ and an outpouring of the Spirit among the sons and daughters, these passages are relegated to the past or into the future after Christ returns.

I call these individuals the "No rain theology crowd." I have studied church history and it is true that from the third century until modern times there was very little true spiritual activity. This is not because the Holy Spirit quit working but because the Christian church began mixing pagan ideas with Christian doctrine. The church became cold, formal and ritualistic. This form of Christianity continued for hundreds of years. Because of the pagan ideas, the formalism and unbelief, the Holy Spirit was unable to bless and minister to the people. There was a dry spell for almost 1800 years. The interesting point is, there is also a dry period from Pentecost to Trumpets!

LIVING FROM PENTECOST TO TRUMPETS

Pentecost usually occurs in the months of May or June. In Israel this begins the hot summer season. I have been to Israel in May when the temperature in the Judean wilderness was 130 degrees. During the four months between Pentecost, the fourth feast, and Trumpets, the fifth feast, there is almost no rain in Israel. As the fall months arrive, Trumpets usually falls in the month of September or October. This is the same season when the rains begin to fall. The clouds are seen forming at first and as the fall months come into the winter it is common to experience large amounts of rain throughout the entire country. Again, this rain is a picture of the rain that helps ripen the fruit of the earth for the coming of Christ (James 5:7).

Since we are living between Pentecost and Trumpets, it stands to reason that the 1900 years of spiritual dryness is a picture of the summer dry season between Pentecost and Trumpets. When I saw this pattern years ago, it helped me to explain to others why there seemed to be a lack of spiritual manifestations from the third century until 1896, when over 100 Baptist members gathered in a Murphy, NC school house. It was there that the Holy Spirit fell upon them and they spoke with tongues and formed a new denomination which later became the Church of God (Cleveland, Tennessee). This was one of the first major outpourings in North America, but only the beginning. The Holy Spirit was poured out in Kansas and in Los Angeles at the famous Azuza Street revival.

As we prophetically move from Pentecost to the Rapture (Trumpets) two things will happen. There will be a major call to repentance to prepare people for the Rapture and the coming Tribulation (pictured through the Day of Atonement). As the church moves closer to the Rapture, just as in the natural realm, the clouds will begin to form to prepare for the rain. The Holy Spirit will prepare for a final outpouring that will climax when the trumpet sounds! The dry spell of summer is breaking as today we are witnessing a global revival of souls and a fresh outpouring of the Spirit flowing from nation to nation! For those who still doubt that the Holy Spirit is for our time, consider this:

Is the death of Christ that occurred at Passover for

us today? Is the act of sanctification from sin, Unleavened Bread, still available today? Is the resurrection at First Fruits still a promise for the dead in Christ for the future? Is the coming of Christ, seen in the Feast of Trumpets, going to occur? Do we still receive forgiveness from sin and judgement as Israel did on the Day of Atonement?

All Christians must answer, "Yes" to the above questions. Then why do some ministers and Christians doubt that the church can experience a continual "Pentecost," from generation to generation? After all, the gifts of the Spirit will continue until the return of Christ.

"So that you come short in no gift, eagerly waiting for the revelation of our Lord Jesus Christ, who will also confirm you to the end, that you may be blameless in the day of our Lord Jesus Christ."
- 1 Corinthians 1:7-8

THE TABERNACLES OUTPOURING

The Feast of Tabernacles is the last of the seven Feasts. This seventh feast occurs in the seventh month and lasts for seven days. It is a reminder of how the children of Israel lived in tents for forty years in the wilderness.

In the days of the Temple, the priests would practice a unique ceremony called the Water Libation Service. This service is an amazing picture of the outpouring of the Holy Spirit. In the time of the Temple four great lamps were erected in the Temple court. These four menorahs had golden cups to hold the olive oil. Four young priests were trained to climb large ladders to the top, carrying immense oil cans holding 120 logs each with which to fill the giant candlesticks. Once lit, there was not a court yard in Jerusalem that did not glow with the light that emanated from the Temple. As the people sang, righteous and pious men would dance before them juggling torches. All of this was to honor the commandment of the water libation.

As the service began the priests would form two rows thirty feet apart carrying twenty-five-foot willow branches. As they would step forward with their right foot, they would wave the branches to the left and visa versa. The waving motion produced a swishing sound like a "rushing wind" (Acts 2:2).

At Tabernacles the men, women, and children all participated. The women stood in the balcony of the court of the women and watched as members of the Sanhedrin danced. The High Priest would later head to the Pool of Siloam with a special vase called the *Mayim Hayim*, or the "living waters." This gold vase would be dipped in the pool and carried with great celebration to the Temple. A second vase made of silver had been filled with wine. As the priest approached the gate, a shofar would be blown as a flute player, called the "pierced one," would begin to play.

After arriving at the Temple the High Priest would pour water into a silver cup on the corner of the brass altar. As he poured water he would quote Scripture:

"For I will pour water on him who is thirsty, and floods on the dry ground. I will pour My Spirit on your descendants, and My blessing on your offspring."
- Isaiah 44:3

OUT OF YOUR BELLY

Jesus was in Jerusalem during the last day of the feast of Tabernacles (John 7:37). The last day of the feast may not have been the seventh day but an additional eighth day that was added on, called *Simchat Torah* or "rejoicing in the Torah." The last day was also when the water libation ceremony occurred. On this day Jesus was standing near the brass altar watching the High Priests pour out the water on the Altar and quoting Scripture.

"On the last day, that great day of the feasts, Jesus stood and cried out, saying, 'If anyone thirsts, let him come to Me and drink. He who believes in Me, as the Scripture has said, out of his heart will flow rivers of living water.' But this He spoke concerning the Spirit, whom those believing in Him would receive; for the Holy Spirit was not yet given, because Jesus was not yet glorified." - John 7:37-39

When the High Priest poured out the living water on the four corners of the altar, it was a perfect picture of God pouring out His Spirit to the north, south, east and west. Jesus knew that the Spirit would be sent to abide in men and therefore used this occasion to announce the outpouring of the Spirit that had not yet come but would come in the future! Since our bodies would become the Temple of the Holy Spirit, Christ knew the power of the Holy Spirit would dwell within man and the power would center in our inner-most being or our "bellies." The area of the belly is the center of the human spirit.

"The spirit of man is the candle of the LORD, searching all the inward parts of the belly."
- Proverbs 20:27 (KJV)

As I said, this yearly event at the Temple, the water libation, was a perfect picture of the Holy Spirit being poured out on all flesh in all nations. This outpouring, coupled with the preaching of the gospel to all nations, will climax with the return of the Messiah (Matthew 24:14). I believe this is why God is releasing so much information about the Hebraic roots of Christianity. It is to prepare the Body of Christ for the return of the Savior and for our 1,000 year rule with Christ in Jerusalem (Revelation 20:4).

ONE LAST THOUGHT

"Then I said, 'Behold, I come; In the scroll of the book it is written of me' " - Psalm 40:7

At the beginning of this book, I wrote to you that I am of the belief that presently books in Heaven are being opened and the ramifications of that are being seen and felt down here on earth. That will continue! I also conveyed to you that the Book, the Bible, is being opened as well - His secrets are being revealed. Ultimately, whether it is books in Heaven or in Earth, it all points to Jesus Christ; it is all written that Christ might be glorified.

That being said, if the only thing you take from this book is information, then you have missed the point. More than information, we are in need of revelation, Christ needs to be revealed to the world as never before.

The things that are coming upon the earth are coming because mankind has consistently turned a deaf ear to His plea to return to Him. This, and His unwillingness to relinquish His Creation to destruction, made it necessary for God to provide a Redeemer - Himself. And so, His Word came and healed our diseases; chief among them being our inherent inclination to sin. It only makes sense then that **He** would be the most consistent and most important "code" found in all of Scripture. He is the sum of it all.

Therefore, if you don't know Him or you don't know Him as you should, then I invite you to remedy that situation right now. Ask Christ to come into your life and change you so that your name will be inscribed in the most important book there is - the Lamb's Book of Life! Amen.

For Additional
Resource Materials
Visit Our Website:

www.perrystone.org

VOICE OF EVANGELISM · P.O. BOX 3595 · CLEVELAND, TN 37320
Phone (423) 478.3456 · Fax (423) 478.1392

Do You Have A Subscription To Voice of Evangelism Magazine?

The VOE magazine is written by Perry Stone, Jr. and mailed out bi-monthly. For a one-time donation of $20, you may receive the magazine for as long as you wish, with no renewal fee. (Please send $30 for subscriptions outside the USA.) The magazine contains Prophecy Updates, Inside the Ministry Updates, Pam's Corner, Feature Articles, and the latest resource products for sale. You will receive six issues a year.

For Credit Card orders call 423.478.3456

For additional resource materials, or to order online, please visit www.perrystone.org

(U.S. FUNDS ONLY)

Paula Deen - Choc Cobler 7-5-10
Pecan

Butter melted
1 C. pecans chopped
1 C. flour
1 C. sugar
1. C. milk
1/2 C. cocoa.

Pecans + cocoa
flour
1 c. water
1